POSTCARDS
from
MANHATTAN

George J. Lankevich

SQUAREONE
PUBLISHERS

Cover Design: Phaedra Mastrocola
In-House Editing: Marie Caratozzolo
Interior Design: Phaedra Mastrocola
Typesetting: Gary A. Rosenberg

Square One Publishers I Garden City Park, NY 11040 I **516-535-2010** I www.squareonepublishers.com

Library of Congress Cataloging-in-Publication Data

Lankevich, George J., 1939–
   Postcards from Manhattan : sights & sentiments from the last century/George J. Lankevich.
     p. cm.
Includes index.
  ISBN 0-7570-0101-7 (quality pbk.)
  1. Manhattan (New York, N.Y.)—History—20th century—Pictorial works. 2. New York (N.Y.)—History—
20th century—Pictorial works. 3. Manhattan (New York, N.Y.)—Social life and customs—20th century—
Pictorial works. 4. New York (N.Y.)—Social life and customs—20th century—Pictorial works. 5. Manhattan
(New York, N.Y.)—History—20th century. 6. New York (N.Y.)—History—20th century. 7. Postcards—
New York (State)—New York. I. Title.
  F128.5 .L24 2002
  974.7'1043—dc21

2002003404

Copyright © 2003 by Square One Publishers

Printed in China

10 9 8 7 6 5 4 3 2 1

Contents

Acknowledgments, v

Introduction, 1

Chapter One | The Tip of the City, 7

• The Statue of Liberty, 11 • City of Immigrants, 13 • Castle Clinton, 16 • Walking on Wall Street, 19
• The Curb Exchange, 23 • George Washington and Federal Hall, 24 • Tribute to the Twin Towers, 26

Chapter Two | Lower Manhattan, 29

• Crossing the Brooklyn Bridge, 37 • Tammany Hall and the Tweed Courthouse, 38 • Life in Greenwich Village, 41
• Washington Square, 44 • Villages in the City, 47 • South Street Seaport, 55

Chapter Three | Midtown Manhattan, 59

• Shopping in Manhattan, 65 • The Flatiron Building, 68 • Garden on the Move, 70
• Giants in the Metropolis, 73 • Rockefeller Center, 82 • Transit Central, 85

Chapter Four   The East Side, 91

• Mansions and Museums, 97   • The Metropolitan Museum of Art, 100
• The Guggenheim Museum, 101

Chapter Five   The West Side, 107

• From Columbus Circle to Columbus Center, 111   • Lincoln Center, 115   • The Ansonia Apartment-Hotel, 117
• Twin Towers of the West Side, 119   • The American Museum of Natural History, 120

Chapter Six   A Walk in Central Park, 125

• Creators of the Park, 133   • Cleopatra's Needle, 141   • Shakespeare in the Park, 144

Chapter Seven   Manhattan Above the Park, 147

The Apollo Theater, 152   • The Second Harlem Renaissance, 157   • Horses and the Speedway, 161
• Grant's Tomb, 162   • The Cathedral of Saint John the Divine, 166   • The Cloisters, 169

Conclusion, 173

The Messages in Print, 175
Index, 177

Acknowledgments

The publisher and author have made every attempt to contact all existing copyright holders. We would like to thank the many postcard dealers and collectors who helped make this book possible. We are especially grateful to the people and organizations who allowed us to use the following postcards:

- The postcards on pages 37, 55, 58, 97, 103, 104, 105, 119, 136, 142, 153, 154, 155, 156, 157, 167, 168, and 171 were reprinted courtesy of the Bob Stonehill Archive.

- The postcard on page 27 was reprinted courtesy of Marisa and Brooke Love.

- The postcards on pages 57, 99, 139, 140, 163, and 164 were reprinted courtesy of the Ron Riemer Collection.

- The postcard on page 43 was reprinted courtesy of Jim Caratozzolo.

- The postcards on pages 13, 34, 50, 69, 85, 96, 118, 122, 123, 141, 151, 159, and 170 were reprinted courtesy of the Al Velocci Collection.

- The postcards on pages 2, 37, 44, 62, and 131 were reprinted courtesy of the Stephen Hoops Collection.

- The postcards on pages 60, 88, 152, and 173 were reprinted courtesy of NewYork.com - www.newyork.com.

- The postcard on page 41 was reprinted courtesy of the Pamela Apkarian-Russell Collection.

Introduction

As planet Earth enters its new millennium, New York reigns as the capital city of the world. Its preeminence is not due to population—other international centers are far larger—or its territory, for its 8 million residents are densely packed into only 326 square miles. Rather, its prominence stems from a century in which it came to symbolize the finest attributes of Western urban culture and the highest stage of capitalist endeavor. The driving force behind this accomplishment was the island of Manhattan.

As the twenty-first century dawns, Manhattan's million and half people, the residents of New York County, continue to reflect the glitter and ambition so long identified with their metropolis. Amazing New York achieved its unrivaled position as the commercial heart of the United States and the financial center of international business, while remaining the world's most ethnically diverse, multi-religious city. Its teeming streets offer both sophistication and slums; they are common ground for moguls and sheiks, artists and artisans, jet setters and immigrants, struggling members of the working class and corporate "Masters of the Universe." Manhattan is *sui generius*—unique; a venue to be experienced and treasured. By combining historical facts with images from authentic postcards bearing personal messages, *Postcards from Manhattan* offers an appreciation of this very special city.

Anything is possible in Manhattan. This fanciful postcard predicts a wilderness of high towers and varied transportation systems. [c.1913]

1

Despite its august position, New York remains strangely available to every person. Multitudes can claim to "know" Manhattan, for its glories have been the subject of innumerable movies and books. Across the world, Wall Street is used as a synonym for capitalism, Broadway means the live theater, Seventh Avenue is equated with fashion, and Madison Avenue connotes the advertising profession. Even Manhattan's neighborhoods have international resonance. Greenwich Village is identified with a bohemian lifestyle, Sutton Place means enormous wealth, the Lower East Side conjures up harsh images of Jewish tenement life, while Hell's Kitchen does the same for Irish dockworkers. Harlem evokes visions of both the Jazz Age and urban pathology. New York is the city with more Jews than Tel Aviv, more Irish than Dublin, more Italians than Naples, and more Puerto Ricans than San Juan. The streets of Manhattan are such an international mixing bowl that after World War II, most diplomats found it impossible to imagine any other city as home to the United Nations.

Peter Minuit and Native Americans

Founded almost four centuries ago by a Dutch trading company and christened New Amsterdam, Manhattan has always attracted ambitious people eager to make money. Business is part of the genetic code of the city, and its unrelenting capitalism invests it with an aggressive aura. Life in Manhattan proceeds at a rapid tempo. As early as the 1640s, its many languages and varied population were already a subject of wonder. Just before the American Revolution, future president John Adams noted how the residents of Manhattan "talk very loud, very fast and altogether," but when he and Abigail later moved from New York, she bitterly lamented having to leave Broadway. During the 1790s, Manhattan served as capital city for both the nation and its state. George Washington was inaugurated president on Wall Street, and the first sessions of both Congress and the Supreme Court were held in the city. Though political centers soon moved elsewhere, business opportunities remained abundant in New York, and were pursued with ferocity.

Manhattan was the largest city in the United States during the nineteenth century. The construction of the Erie Canal in 1825 guaranteed that the trade of the interior continent would flow into the metropolis through the only geographic break in the Appalachian Mountains. By mid-century, Manhattan handled more goods than all other American ports combined—fully two-thirds of national exports and a third of imports. Already the small island at the mouth of the Hudson River possessed a legendary quality as the land of opportunity, and was the primary destination for unending waves of immigrants seeking a better life. Although it is certain that not all the newcomers were successful, they added immensely to the human capital of the city. Generations of Irish, German, Italian, Jewish, Chinese, Dominican, Vietnamese, and dozens of other immigrant groups have followed their dreams to the "North Star" of Manhattan. No temporary difficulty, from the Civil War to economic collapse to racial animosity to terrorism, has ever stemmed the tide of immigrants whose presence makes Manhattan an ever-changing kaleidoscope.

By 1898, when Manhattan united with Brooklyn, Queens, the Bronx, and Staten Island to form the City of Greater New York, the image and reality of the metropolis was well established. Geographic expansion made possible a population that now exceeds 8 million; but, to this day, residents of four outer boroughs still refer to Manhattan as "the City." Such deference is not misplaced, because Manhattan, an island barely more than 13 miles long and only 2.3 miles across at its widest, has always been the economic heart of the metropolis. Yet despite its long prominence, much of the island remained undeveloped in 1898. Consolidation provided the incentive to fill in unsettled portions of its terrain. Well-established neighborhoods such as Greenwich Village, the Lower East Side, and Harlem were soon augmented by newer districts such as Times Square, the Upper East Side, and Morningside Heights. On the busy wharves of the Fulton Street Market, amid the canyons of Wall Street and new apartment complexes on the West Side, in the bright lights of Broadway and the gritty reality of 125th Street, the legend of the "city that never sleeps" was created.

Manhattan became a metropolis of many peoples, a chaos that was constantly changing and infinitely challenging. Justly famous as the citadel of the skyscraper, Manhattan appeared ever ready to tear down its past and eliminate part of its history in the firm conviction that it could build something better tomorrow. The city ignored criticism, established its own rules, encouraged free spirits, and constantly

Manhattan's ever-changing kaleidoscope is apparent in Herald Square. Once the heart of the city's red-light Tenderloin district, it became an upscale destination at the turn of the twentieth century, when a newspaper, hotels, and Macy's department store opened there. [c.1912]

redefined the nature of success. Throughout the twentieth century, Manhattan became the most influential business, commercial, and artistic center on earth. *Postcards from Manhattan* features some of the many faces Manhattan has presented to an awed world.

An entire library of histories chronicles the amazing story of New York, but prose often fails to convey the color, vibrancy, and glamour of Manhattan. Indelible memories were common currency on that island, and we are fortunate that so many images have been captured in one of the nation's most unpretentious historical records—the simple picture postcard.

Although they were not invented in the United States, postcards became an almost ubiquitous way of marking national achievements during the "American Century." Proud citizens first began to send photographic memories during Chicago's Colombian Exposition of 1893, and soon *deltiology*—the collection and study of postcards—became a popular hobby. The modern split-back postal card did not make its appearance until 1907, a year when over a billion cards were sold annually. According to the postal service, 667 million cards were actually delivered in 1908 as the mania for collecting cards and sharing images became more widespread. It is a simple truth that for generations, sending a postcard was the most efficient way for travelers to inform relatives and friends of their

Central Park's Swan Pond

doings. Messages on cards cost less to mail than a letter, saved time, and trumpeted the fact that senders were in a place everyone dreamed about visiting. Enterprising companies offered views of most major American cities, but no urban center was as popular among postcard collectors as Manhattan. People passing through Manhattan, foreign visitors, and proud residents of the city all used the postcard as a means to "keep in touch." As a result, we possess a unique historical record of the expansion of Manhattan during the course of the twentieth century—visual testimony to its greatness.

Collectors of postcards, whether in 1901 or 2001, have always been fascinated by representations of New York. Although the form and style of postal art has changed over time, Manhattan's rise to world prominence remains an infinitely enticing subject. Postcards that were printed abroad dominated the early decades of the last century, but American firms created most of the "linen" and "chrome" cards sold from World War I to the 1960s. Economic forces then shifted production overseas. Regardless of the source, however, Manhattan's images were always prized by both collectors and the general public. New York was the national metropolis, Manhattan was its vibrant heart, and Tom, Dick, or Mary visited there. The pace of the city was overwhelming, its buildings fantastic, and the style of its inhabitants difficult to fathom—the personal commentaries written on postcards make these points continually. But it was the pictures on the fronts of these cards that made it clear why Manhattan remained a mecca for every American.

In 1898, New York was almost three centuries old, but many parts of Manhattan would have been recognizable to famed city residents such as Washington Irving, Clement Clarke Moore, Aaron Burr, and Herman Melville. During the 1900s, this city experienced violent and continuous change, both in its infrastructure and population, and altered itself many times. Postcards enable us to recapture some of the essence of nineteenth-century Manhattan, and trace the twentieth-century alterations that transformed it into the biggest, the most envied, and the most dynamic urban center in America. The face of the city underwent change—its famed diversity expanded; its confident citizens displayed boorish behavior as often as brilliance; its buildings soared and metropolitan wealth grew.

Times Square in the early 1900s.

Postcards from Manhattan documents the ever-changing reality of this most interesting city, a record captured by a host of past images. Its pages combine a pictorial odyssey through Manhattan's evolving cityscape with information on city history and modern attractions. Neither words nor pictures pretend to be complete, but together they spur recognition of the city's uniqueness. Beginning at the harbor where the Dutch first settled, this volume chronicles the northward advance of the city. While trade and finance still dominate the southern edge of the island, modern Manhattan offers its many visitors far more than commerce. Successive chapters show the development of city neighborhoods as well as visitor-friendly Midtown. Beyond the East Side and West Side, readers will learn why areas such as Central Park and the areas north of 110th Street all contribute to Manhattan's allure. The "city that never sleeps" is, in reality, dozens of neighborhoods where ordinary people live out the rhythm of their daily lives. Their efforts, dreams, and talents continue to provide the bedrock that makes New York the world's great metropolis.

Attempting to summarize the city's paradoxes, a wondering reporter analyzed it as "a wilderness of human flesh; crazed with avarice, lust and rum," and concluded that Manhattan's true name was "delirium." But he was wrong. Under the constantly changing surface, there exists solidity and order, pattern and control. Living in Manhattan challenges everyone, but the island is a spectacular success continually refining itself. Hopefully, the postcard images that record its story will provide just as much pleasure to the viewer as they did to collectors. 🐌

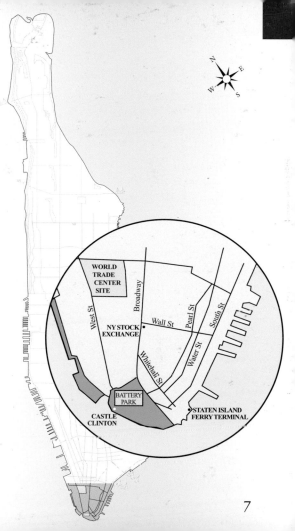

CHAPTER ONE
The Tip of the City

The saga of Manhattan begins with water. It is impossible to consider the history of the city without reference to the many waterways that surround it and determine its character. Manhattan is a small island located at the head of a vast bay, and the contemporary world provides no sight more thrilling than the man-made mountains of concrete that spring up out of New York Harbor. The natural vista was perhaps equally entrancing to explorers such as Giovanni da Verrazano and Henry Hudson when they first sailed into the bay's protected waters. After passage through the mile-wide entrance of The Narrows, these adventurers viewed one of the world's finest natural harbors, a vast anchorage that seemed eager to accept the commerce of the world. The Dutch Republic fully appreciated the possibilities it offered, and in 1624, established a trading post on the southern tip of Manahatta (as the island was called in a Spanish document) in hopes of tapping the resources of the North American continent. The settlement was called New Amsterdam after 1625, although it did not receive autonomous city status until 1653.

Trade and commerce were the primary concerns of the Dutch West India Company and the settlers it dispatched. Farms, windmills, and taverns soon appeared in the new town, but it was the availability of furs—the first of many trade items that Manhattan would send into the world—that brought prosperity. In 1626, resident Director

7

Peter Minuit purchased the entire island from Native Americans supposedly for $24 worth of trinkets. At least three Manhattan sites claim to be the place where history's greatest real estate deal was finalized, but scholars note that the tribes who sold the land had no authority to do so, and may have actually swindled the Dutch.

Whatever the truth of a contract now shrouded by time, growing New Amsterdam focused commercial activity along its eastern shoreline rather than under the high bluffs that ran along the Hudson River. Over the next three centuries, men would gradually level the geography and expand the city further into the harbor by creating landfill. Several hundred blocks of modern Manhattan's valuable land are the result of this systematic triumph over nature. It is on this man-made territory that the city conducts much of the business that is the foundation of its wealth. Today, Water and West Streets, which marked the original shoreline, are well inland, while Hudson Street to the north is fully four blocks from the river it once watched. From colonial days to the present, speculating in real estate has been the key element in many Manhattan fortunes.

Walking through the modern Financial District and Battery Park offers little evidence of the 160 years when Manhattan existed under Dutch and English authority, although the cobblestones of the Stone Street Historic District manage to evoke a past age. Battery

Battery Park

Park, located at the tip of Manhattan, holds several monuments that honor the nautical heritage of the metropolis. Many people take the ferry from the park to Staten Island so they can pass in front of the Statue of Liberty, perhaps the greatest symbol of America and a beacon that drew millions of immigrants to the United States. On the Battery itself, the massive bulk of Castle Clinton—originally a fort constructed to protect the city from British invasion in 1812; Governor's Island—a military post since the Washington administration and still a source of development controversy; and Pier A from the Victorian Era—long a site for fireboats and home to a Merchant Marine Memorial, each testify to Manhattan's intimate relationship with the sea.

Bowling Green, the first park in the city, is dominated by the huge Customs House, a 1907 structural gem that was designed by architect Cass Gilbert. Today, this building honors the memory of New York's Alexander Hamilton, first Secretary of the Treasury, and houses the National Museum of the American Indian. Customs taxes seem terribly old-fashioned to modern citizens, but until passage of the Income Tax Amendment in 1913, the tariff duties collected in Manhattan were the primary source of national revenue. The area around the green is the oldest section of Manhattan, and parts of the island's past are lovingly preserved there.

On Pearl Street, which once marked the shoreline, is found

Fraunces Tavern, a colonial alehouse reconstructed in the twentieth century to provide a link to New York's revolutionary past. In 1783, General Washington bade farewell to his loyal officers there, and its "Long Room" Museum still seems to resonate with the presence of the Father of this country.

North of the Battery begin the blocks of high buildings that make Manhattan famous, a veritable forest of skyscrapers. Lower Broadway is the site where American heroes such as Charles Lindbergh and U.S. astronauts, as well as championship New York sports teams, have been welcomed with ticker-tape parades—world-famous celebrations unique to the city. Both the size of the structures in this "Canyon of Heroes" and their confetti snowstorms indicate the financial power that resides in Manhattan.

Only a few blocks up Broadway lies Wall Street, which was the northern extent of Manhattan in 1653, when Governor Peter Stuyvesant ordered construction of a barricade to protect the city from attacks. Now only the Bulls and the Bears wage battle in that area, which has been the financial capital of the nation since the early nineteenth century. Yet even in the heart of capitalism, Manhattan's link to water is apparent, for directly to the west are the ninety-two acres of landfill that have become Battery Park City, home to 40,000 persons and a "Riviera on the Hudson," from which walkers can contemplate the sea. This vast development replaced rotting nineteenth-century piers, and demonstrates the city's amazing ability to reinvent itself every generation. It is this constant renewal that makes Manhattan endlessly enticing. ᕗ

Fort Amsterdam

New York City Hall

Bird's-Eye View of Lower New York,

Copyright 1905 Illustrated Postal Card Co. N.Y.

96-119

The extraordinary activity of New York Harbor, including liners, ferry boats, and sailing ships, is evident in this early twentieth-century postcard. The great East River bridges are visible in the background. [c.1914]

The Statue of Liberty

In 1865, France suffered under the increasingly authoritarian rule of Napoleon III. At a dinner party hosted by Edouard-René de Laboulaye, guests developed the idea of presenting a statue to the United States to celebrate American liberty, a gift that would also remind Frenchmen of their own heritage. Sculptor Frédéric Auguste Bartholdi was commissioned to produce a model entitled "Liberty Enlightening the World."

When Bartholdi visited the United States in 1871, he sailed past Bedloe's Island in the harbor and envisioned his statue there. With funding provided by the French-American Union, the inspired Alsatian expanded the height of his model from 4 feet to 151 feet. Bartholdi's task took years. One finished section, the statue's hand and torch, was displayed at the 1876 Philadelphia Centennial and then in Manhattan's Madison Square Park, while the head became an attraction at the Paris Universal Exposition in 1878. French engineer Alexandre Gustave Eiffel was recruited to build an internal framework that was capable of supporting 100 tons of copper sheathing and standing up to the winds of New York Bay. Without its strong iron skeleton, "Liberty" would have been propelled up the Hudson River.

It was America's responsibility to prepare Bedloe's Island and construct a suitable pedestal for the gift that France presented the American Ambassador in 1884. But both Congress and the New York legislature declined to fund the project. It was Manhattan's Union League Club, along with various other groups, that raised enough money for architect Richard Morris Hunt to design and build the statue's foundation and base. When cash ran short, the last $121,000 was contributed by 120,000 ordinary citizens of Manhattan.

"Liberty" arrived in 214 crates in June 1885. Her reconstruction began that November, and President Grover Cleveland dedicated her on October 28, 1886. Paris kept two smaller versions of Lady Liberty, but the only full-sized statue reigns in New York Harbor to welcome millions of immigrants and visitors to Manhattan. During a major rehabilitation in the 1980s, a rebuilt torch, new windows, and steel armature replacing Eiffel's corroded ironwork were installed. Rededicated on July 4, 1986, the world's largest metal statue and probably its single most famous sculpture provides tourists with a magnificent view of lower Manhattan.

Visited by over 4 million people annually, the "Lady in the Harbor" remains the most vibrant symbol of American freedom. [c.1943]

ELLIS ISLAND—IMMIGRATION DEPOT, NEW YORK.

Here we are first landing from Ireland. M.J.F.

Ellis Island, where the "dreams and tears" of over 12 million immigrants first encountered America, is a revered national shrine. Restoration of its Main Registry Building was the largest historic renovation in American history. [c.1905]

City of Immigrants

New York has always been a city that welcomed immigration, an urban mosaic whose Babel of languages was constantly augmented by the influx of peoples from around the globe. Manhattan's tradition of accepting newcomers began in colonial times when Peter Stuyvesant attempted to expel some newly arrived Brazilian Jews in 1654. The directors of the Dutch West India Company ordered their incredulous governor to grant the Jews all civil and political rights, including the privilege of constructing a synagogue. A chastised Stuyvesant changed his attitude and authorized a Jewish burial ground near modern Chatham Square. Religious toleration was further enhanced when the town of Flushing specifically guaranteed "liberty of conscience" to all residents, including Quakers, in 1657. Manhattan's future history would show occasional instances of bigotry, but the official tradition of religious and ethnic freedom that was articulated in colonial times has remained a constant value in city life.

By 1822, novelist James Fenimore Cooper asserted that Manhattan "is composed of inhabitants from all the countries of Christendom." Large numbers of Scots, Welsh, French, and Germans were present among its 125,000 people, but in truth, the city was still dominated by English and Dutch stock. Yet over the next century, some 35 million persons would emigrate to the United States, and three quarters of them would pass through Manhattan. The first great wave—refugees from the potato blight in Ireland—began to arrive in 1845. Both poor and Catholic, the Irish influx fostered a vicious nativist movement, and signs across the city advised that "No Irish Need Apply" for jobs. In spite of this, they continued to come in ever-increasing numbers. Necessity soon forced the city to convert Castle Garden—a recreation hub that was once the fortress Castle Clinton—into an immigrant reception center. Economic growth was so rapid that the Irish were able to find jobs in construction and on the docks. By 1860, half of Manhattan's 800,000 people were foreign born, and the city was the largest city in the Western Hemisphere.

Until the 1880s, immigration to the United States came largely from western and northern Europe, but then the flow shifted towards the southern and eastern sections of the continent. Jews fled Russian

Under the tiled vault of the Registry Hall, immigrants prepared to enter the United States; 80 percent spent less than a day on Ellis Island. [c.1908]

pogroms, while Italians, Greeks, and Slavs ran from poverty. To deal with this "new immigration," the government opened Ellis Island on January 1, 1892, as a larger reception center. Named for a revolutionary merchant who ran a fisherman's tavern there, the island was once used as an execution site for pirates. Before it was closed in 1954, Ellis Island processed 12 million steerage passengers seeking a new life in the United States. Wealthier immigrants were examined onboard ship and never experienced Ellis.

The first immigrant accepted at Ellis Island was Annie Moore of County Cork, Ireland, who lived most of her life in Waco, Texas; but millions of other "Annies" settled in Manhattan. Before winning admission to the city, over 2 million received some form of medical attention in the hospital that was adjacent to Ellis's main reception hall. Genealogists estimated in the year 2000 that 40 percent of present-day citizens can trace their antecedents to Ellis Island. When the Museum of Immigration, located there since 1992, opened a website in 2001, it was quickly overrun with inquiries.

Ellis Island is presently part of the Statue of Liberty National Monument, and a much-visited site. The statue itself, a vital symbol of freedom in its earliest years, gradually acquired a second role in the twentieth century as the "Mother of Exiles." A key part of that transformation was Emma Lazarus' "The New Colossus," a poem written in 1883 to raise funds for the pedestal. In 1903, a bronze plaque was placed at the base of "Miss Liberty" welcoming the "tired . . . poor . . . huddled masses yearning to breathe free."

Despite terrible stories of families separated by illness, of insensitive bureaucrats who changed surnames, and of refugees detained in sight of the mainland, the vast majority of immigrants spent less than six hours on Ellis Island before entering Manhattan. The stream slowed only when Congress passed restrictive legislation in 1924. After 1954, Ellis Island was used as a Coast Guard training station, an alien deportation center, a veterans hospital, and a depot for displaced persons. Gradually, its structures fell into disrepair. But in 1990, its main building was rehabilitated and, as part of the Museum of Immigration, it now welcomes millions of visitors annually.

New federal laws in 1965 and 1986 encouraged immigration, and much of the energy generated by contemporary New York City is supplied by Latin and Asian newcomers. Dominicans, Russians, and Chinese constitute the largest incoming groups, and every new arrival seems to embrace the city "with the intense excitement of first love."

The influx of the 1990s allowed the boroughs of the Greater City to surpass 8 million in population in the year 2000, although Manhattan's population remained stagnant. Due to increasing immigration, the city is now 40 percent foreign born. City schools count 196 ethnic groups, and non-Hispanic whites comprise only 35 percent of the total population; there are more Latins than blacks, and Asians populate three separate Chinatowns.

The marvelous ability of New York to assimilate immigrants and transform them into Americans is forever evident in this contemporary city.

535

AQUARIUM, (Formerly Castle Garden) BATTERY PARK and WHITEHALL BL'DG.
NEW YORK

Castle Clinton, always a powerful presence on Manhattan's Battery waterfront, has provided defensive, entertainment, and immigration services to the city. An aquarium from 1896 to 1941, it drew 76 million visitors; in 1946, it was declared a national monument. [c.1915]

Castle Clinton

Early in the nineteenth century, the fledgling United States faced the possibility of a second war with Great Britain, and a frenzy of "fortification fever" swept American urban centers. In New York, four forts that were intended to repel invasion rose quickly, including one called the West Battery on a small island almost 200 feet off the southern tip of Manhattan. Designed by architect John McComb, the three-story structure featured ramparts eight feet thick, held twenty-eight guns, and was renamed Castle Clinton in 1815 in honor of DeWitt Clinton, the city's wartime mayor. Although its cannons were never fired in anger, the fort played a prominent role in Manhattan's development.

In July of 1824, Castle Clinton was decommissioned; the building was taken over by private management and renamed Castle Garden. The former fortress became a site for concerts, political and business receptions, and simple promenades atop its wide walls. Foreign dignitaries such as the Marquis de Lafayette and Hungarian leader Louis Kossuth were entertained there, as were several sitting presidents. Opera performances began at the Castle Garden in 1845, and the musical event of the century—P.T. Barnum's presentation of Jenny Lind—took place there on September 11, 1850.

Landfill eventually connected Castle Garden to the mainland, and it began a new career as an immigrant landing station in 1855. Over the next thirty-five years, more than 7.5 million immigrants were processed there and released into Manhattan, where they immediately encountered "runners" and "steerers" who either helped or preyed on the newcomers. After Castle Garden closed in 1840,

immigrants came through the Barge office before Ellis Island opened in 1892.

In 1896, the architectural firm of McKim, Mead and White transformed Castle Garden into the New York Aquarium. When Robert Moses, the premier builder of New York, proposed destruction of the facility to construct an approach to the Battery Tunnel, public opinion dealt him a rare defeat. Castle Clinton was declared a national monument on August 12, 1946, and under the administration of the National Park Service, still provides the public with unrivaled views of the harbor.

Castle Clinton—still enchanting to modern-day tourists. [c. 1910]

New Custom House.

Built on the site of Dutch Fort Amsterdam (and perhaps the place where Manhattan Island was purchased), Cass Gilbert's Customs House now magnificently houses the National Museum of the American Indian. It overlooks Bowling Green, Manhattan's first public park. [c.1910]

FRAUNCES' TAVERN   NEW YORK

BROAD AND PEARL STS.

GENERAL WASHINGTON'S FAREWELL TO HIS OFFICERS

On the 4th of December, 1783, General Washington bade the officers of the Continental Army goodby while in Fraunces' Tavern, corner of Broad and Pearl Streets, New York City. Filling a glass with wine, after the ceremonious fashion of the time, he said: "With a heart full of love and gratitude, I now take leave of you. I most earnestly wish that your latter days may be as prosperous and happy as your former ones have been glorious and honorable. I can not come to each of you and take my leave, but shall be obliged to you, if each of you will come to me and take me by the hand." 'Twas a sad time to those assembled. Washington left the room, passing through the Light Infantry, and walked to the river where he got into a boat, and waving his hat to his old friends, moved away for the Jersey shore. He journeyed to Annapolis, resigned his commission and returned to Mount Vernon.—From the writings of Park Custis, by Mr. Joseph I. Keefer, of D. C.

SOUVENIR POST CARD CO. N. Y.

Innkeeper Samuel Fraunces presided over Manhattan's finest inn from 1762 to 1785, and later served as steward for President Washington. This postcard shows the restaurant/museum as restored in Colonial Revival style. The complex is listed on the National Register of Historic Places. [c.1910]

Walking on Wall Street

Few phrases evoke such strong reactions as "Wall Street," words that for almost two centuries have conjured up images of capitalist bankers, predatory investors of obscene wealth, and dreams of easy living. From its very origins, Wall Street was identified with protection. Dutch New Amsterdam had made it the site of a palisade that stretched across the island—a defense against Indian assault or invasion from New England, neither of which ever occurred. The wall itself vanished by the 1680s. As the city's population gradually moved north, residences sprang up on Wall Street, and the Episcopal Parish of Trinity was built at the head of the street facing the waters of the Hudson River. Almost a century later, the bulk of Manhattan's population was still found south of Wall Street, and City Hall was located there as well.

Located on the "broad way" leading out of Manhattan, Trinity Church has watched Wall Street for over three centuries. [c.1895]

Only at the end of the eighteenth century did Wall Street begin its long association with financial trading. In 1768, Manhattan had founded the first Chamber of Commerce in the New World, but the nation's first stock exchange was organized in Philadelphia in 1790. Jealous Manhattan brokers created their own exchange two years later by signing the Butternut Agreement on May 17, 1792. The newly formed New York Stock and Exchange Board was ineffective, but its members continued to congregate and confer at the Tontine Coffee House on Wall and Water Streets. Even after reorganization in 1817, the Board remained less important than Philadelphia's, and would stay that way until the 1830s. In that decade, Manhattan's growing control over western commerce, its essential role in marketing southern cotton, and President Andrew Jackson's assault on the Second Bank of the United States shifted financial power to New York, where it has remained ever since. Wall Street became "a block of money between a graveyard [Trinity] and a river." It was Manhattan's "street of dreams."

During the Civil War, as the national debt soared, the New York Stock Exchange (NYSE) became the primary arena in which debt and stocks were marketed. A world without financial security laws made possible the flamboyant careers of men such as Jim Fisk, Daniel Drew, and "Commodore" Cornelius Vanderbilt. But the governing leaders of the NYSE gradually established trading rules that eliminated much financial piracy and made possible the vast expansion of the American economy in the nineteenth century. Great banking houses, such as that of J. Pierpont Morgan, located themselves on Wall Street and financed railroads, utilities, and steel-making plants. The "House of Morgan" was so powerful that it was able to deal with the national economic panics that occurred in 1893 and 1907. Its headquarters at 23 Wall Street was known simply as "The Corner." On September 16, 1920, the Corner was victimized by a bomb explosion in which thirty people were killed—a crime that was never solved.

The constant ups and downs of Wall Street culminated in the Great Crash of October 24, 1929, after which hotel clerks supposedly asked room patrons if they were registering for "sleeping or jumping." In time, the market recovered and the NYSE remained its vital center. Only the outbreak of World War I and the September 11, 2001 attack on the World Trade Center in Manhattan closed the Exchange, which continues to set the financial tone for the world.

The pageant of Wall Street is incomplete without considering its second great institution—Trinity Church. The English Conquest of Manhattan in 1664 installed Anglicanism as the official religion of the province, but not until 1697 was Trinity's congregation large enough to merit a royal charter from King William. The present church is one of very few American institutions still governed by a royal decree. Trinity's graveyard is the final resting place for many prominent Americans, including William Bradford, Alexander Hamilton, Francis Lewis, and Robert Fulton. Queen Anne's patronage awarded Trinity an important land grant in 1705, which became the basis for its great wealth.

Over the next two centuries, Trinity became known as the "Mother of Churches," contributing generously to establish Anglican parishes in New England and New York, building satellite chapels in Manhattan, founding a school, and providing social services. Among the many institutions it helped create was Kings College in 1754, now world famous as Columbia University. The present Trinity Church—the third to stand on the site and the first to face Wall Street—was designed by architect Richard Upjohn in neo-Gothic style and opened in 1846. For almost fifty years, its steeple was the tallest structure in Manhattan. Until 1905, when the celebration moved to Times Square, Trinity's "ring" of ten bells drew hundreds of island residents annually to greet the New Year.

After 300 years, Queen Anne's small land grant has become the basis for a real estate empire that funds Trinity's mission work, charities, and upkeep. When Queen Elizabeth II visited Manhattan to help celebrate America's bicentennial, the church presented her with 279 peppercorns—the annual "quitrent" due since its chartering. This is certainly quite a bargain, for contemporary Trinity boasts debt-free ownership of twenty-five office towers in lower Manhattan that return annual revenues in excess of $120 million. It seems eminently fitting that the world's richest parish should preside over the world's money center.

The trading floor of the Stock Exchange is one of the busiest and most intimidating places on earth. Behind its classical façade, there exists daily chaos as fortunes are made and lost. [c.1965]

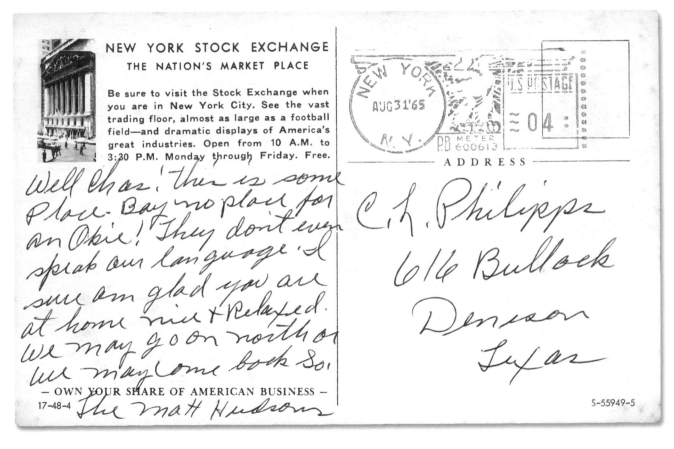

NEW YORK STOCK EXCHANGE
THE NATION'S MARKET PLACE

Be sure to visit the Stock Exchange when you are in New York City. See the vast trading floor, almost as large as a football field—and dramatic displays of America's great industries. Open from 10 A.M. to 3:30 P.M. Monday through Friday. Free.

— OWN YOUR SHARE OF AMERICAN BUSINESS —

17-48-4

S-55949-5

Well Chas! this is some Place. Bay no place for an Okie! They don't even speak our language. I sure am glad you are at home nice & Relaxed. We may go on north or we may come back So. The Matt Hudsons

NEW YORK
AUG 31 '65
N. Y.

P.B METER
P.B 600613

U.S POSTAGE
04

ADDRESS

C. L. Philipps
616 Bullock
Denison
Texas

The Curb Exchange

Manhattan's creation of the Stock and Exchange Board in the 1790s brought the first glimmerings of order to the hazardous and chaotic world of investment. As the board matured into the New York Stock Exchange (NYSE), it looked down upon the less successful brokers and businesses, which were not permitted to enter its sanctuary. Yet for a century after the NYSE was established, poor but honest brokers, struggling firms rich only in ideas and hope, and fly-by-night speculators provided competition to the establishment in the more hospitable surroundings of "the Curb" outside the exchange.

Gambling in riskier enterprises and calm in the face of short-sale manipulations, Curb Exchange dealers did a great volume of business that often surpassed the primary marketplace. Despised as "guttersnipes" by larger brokerages, they traded in western mines, watered-down railroads, and new manufacturing plants as long as there was daylight. The younger brokers on the Curb were as quick on their feet as they were glib with their promises.

Not until early in the twentieth century was a more formal organization imposed upon the hordes outside the NYSE. A directory of reliable brokers in 1904 and a constitution in 1911 brought stability to its transactions, although those who insisted on gambling in stocks made use of hidden "bucket shops" for another two decades. Genteel respectability came when the Curb Exchange moved indoors in 1921, but it remained the primary path for smaller yet innovative firms to win a position in Manhattan's vicious marketplace. Over the years, many of these firms achieved both wealth and a NYSE listing.

Since 1953, the Curb has been called the American Stock Exchange (AMEX). It ranks as the second largest securities market in the nation.

Broad Street showing Curb brokers, New York

Rules were few on the Curb, and parties to a dispute often found it necessary to retain a biased judge as well as a lawyer. [c.1899]

George Washington and Federal Hall

In December 1783, when George Washington bade farewell to his officers at Fraunces Tavern, he never expected to return to Manhattan. Yet little more than five years later, as the newly elected President of the United States, he made a triumphal procession north from Mount Vernon to assume office in America's first capital city. A specially made barge brought Washington from New Jersey to the Battery, and Governor George Clinton escorted him to a house on Cherry Street, which served as the presidential mansion.

After a week of festivities, Washington traveled to Manhattan's City Hall, a building remodeled by Pierre L'Enfant to serve as the nation's capitol building. April 30, 1789 was a gray and cold day, and after Vice President John Adams presented him to the Congress, it was a sober Washington, dressed in American homespun cloth, who stepped onto the balcony before a hushed crowd. He took the oath of office from New York Chancellor Robert Livingstone—the highest judge available, since no federal judiciary had yet been established. The first president then kissed his Masonic Bible, a flag fluttered to the top of the capitol's cupola, and the bells of every Manhattan church began to ring. The United States was born, and Washington stepped inside the building to deliver his short inaugural. Afterwards, everyone walked north to Saint Paul's Chapel for a service of thanksgiving.

Manhattan's tenure as the national capital ended in 1790. The City Hall where Washington took office reverted to its original use, but the ever-growing city would soon eliminate all traces of these historic events. After a new City Hall was built in 1811, the building in which the president and Congress had consulted was sold for $425; the Cherry Street presidential mansion was later razed to build the Brooklyn Bridge. In 1842, Ithiel Town and A.J. Davis designed a Customs House for the Federal Hall site, a Doric Greek Revival structure that became the busiest place in the nation's greatest port for twenty years. In 1862, the building was remodeled to serve as the United States Sub-Treasury, and did so until 1925.

Today, the Federal Hall National Monument is revered as among the most historic places in the entire city. Although damaged by the terrorist attack of September 11, 2001, it provided shelter to hundreds. Repaired and refurbished, Federal Hall hosted a joint session of Congress on September 6, 2002.

John Quincy Adams Ward's imposing statue of George Washington, which gazes toward the New York Stock Exchange from the steps of Federal Hall, has presided over Wall Street since 1883. [c.1909]

GREATER NEW YORK
WALL STREET

Standard Oil Building, Bowling Green, New York City.

Federal Reserve Bank Building, New York City.

Two impressive structures illuminate competing forces in Manhattan's marketplace. The Standard Oil Building (left) displays the power and wealth of corporate America. [c.1925] The Federal Reserve Bank Building (right) solidly implies the government's desire to control both money and capitalism. [c.1920]

Tribute to the Twin Towers

New York has reigned as America's international marketplace and financial leader since the 1830s, but only with the construction of the Twin Towers of the World Trade Center did it acquire a dominant site dedicated to global commerce. As early as 1946, the legislature chartered a World Trade Center Corporation, but little was accomplished until banker David Rockefeller became convinced that all lower Manhattan would be revived by completing such a complex. The political clout of David's brother, Governor Nelson Rockefeller, convinced the Port Authority to expand its mandate beyond transportation. Preparations for the construction of two colossal buildings began in the mid-1960s and the project took eight years to complete.

Everything about the Twin Towers (called David and Nelson by some critics) was stupendous. The foundation of the sixteen-acre site lay 70 feet below ground level, and a "bathtub" wall over 3,100 feet long was constructed to keep out the subterranean streams and the Hudson River. The earth that was removed for the foundation created nearly 24 acres of new Manhattan real estate on which Liberty Park and Battery Park City would rise.

Architect Minoura Yamasaki designed two "minimalist" buildings—hollow tubes with load-bearing exterior frames that were capable of resisting stress and wind—destined to rise over a quarter mile. The concrete used in the structures could have paved a highway to Washington DC, while the steel could have built three additional Brooklyn Bridges. Ironically, Yamasaki was afraid of heights, so the windows he designed were quite small; but there were 43,600 of them, using 600,000 square feet of glass. The core of each building contained 239 elevator banks with 20,000 doors; the fastest car traveled upwards at 27 feet a second. To service hundreds of corporations and 50,000 workers there were 49,000 tons of air-conditioning equipment, over 30,000 miles of electrical/phone cables, and a seventy-five-store shopping mall.

Dedicated in April 1973, the southern tower rose to a height of 1,362 feet; its brother to the north reached 1,368 feet and was topped with a TV antenna. Each tower had its own zip code. Years passed before they were fully rented, but when the Port Authority sold the towers in 2001, it netted $3.25 billion.

The Twin Towers of the World Trade Center were the ultimate New York skyscrapers. [c.1975]

Despite their monumental statistics, the towers were always more functional office space than beloved buildings. Critics labeled them "General Motors Gothic," and mocked their boxy nature. Tour guides were known to tell visitors the best thing about the forty-five-mile view from the south tower's observation deck was that "You can't see the towers."

It took the tragedy of September 11, 2001, to show how intertwined the Twin Towers had become with the image of Manhattan. They had appeared in so many movies and postcards that their place in the skyline seemed immutable. The terrorist attack left a hole in the picture and an ache in the heart of America. The city may rebuild the site, but there will never be another such complex.

Manhattan, magnificently illuminated across the East River, gives the appearance of an amusement park whose lights can attract the whole world. For over a century, its skyline has been a global icon. [c.1939]

CHAPTER TWO
*L*ower Manhattan

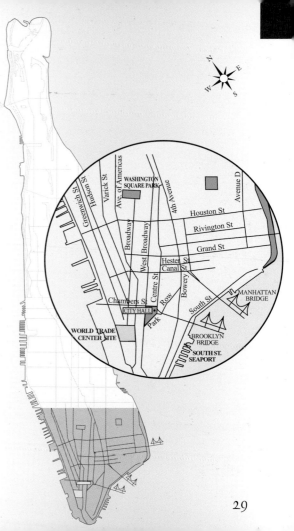

*L*ower Manhattan—the area extending from Wall Street to 14th Street—contains some of the most important businesses in the world; it is also home to some of the city's long-established neighborhoods. A good way to obtain a sense of the area is to stand within City Hall Park, turn in a slow circle, and experience several centuries of metropolitan change. To the south stand the modern skyscrapers of the financial district. Here are found citadels of capitalism, such as the Stock Exchange, the former United States Customs House, and the Federal Reserve Bank, where $66 billion in gold bullion is kept on deposit. Until September 11, 2001, the famous Twin Towers of the World Trade Center were also on display.

Rotating one's gaze westward, the eyes are brought down to earth by Saint Paul's Chapel, an eighteenth-century relic that has served New Yorkers since 1766. After his inauguration, George Washington attended a prayer service there, and visitors can still see the pew in which he knelt. Nearby is the massive bulk of the Woolworth Building, a "cathedral of commerce" built in 1913 to show the vast success that sales of five and ten cents can bring to merchants.

Merely three blocks to the north at Chambers and Broadway, Alexander T. Stewart built his grand "Marble Palace" in 1846. Stewart's, the world's first true department store, set the tone for Manhattan retailing for generations, but Woolworth's

29

five-and-dime revolution at the turn of the century was equally important. Together, the two sites are a reminder that commerce is the vital blood of Manhattan.

Located directly north of the viewer is City Hall, one of the most important buildings in America and the civic and political center of Manhattan. Constructed between 1803 and 1812, it is a grace note of the past amidst a group of modern structures. Designed by John McComb and Joseph F. Mangin, the structure has been almost entirely rebuilt over the decades, yet retains its beauty. When it was originally built, City Hall was so far uptown, that its northern side was left unmarbled because no one was expected to see it. This is one of the few times that Manhattan's ambition seemed willing to accept a limited future. Immediately behind City Hall's lovely elegance lies the infamous "Tweed Courthouse," an architecturally distinguished monument that was the brainchild of the Democratic "Boss" William Marcy Tweed, and a building that provides the nation with an enduring symbol of city machine politics. Proceeding east along Chambers Street brings walkers to the city archives and the massive Municipal Building, designed by architects McKim, Mead and White. It is a marvelously decorated structure that straddles a major thoroughfare and houses many city agencies. Beyond it are found the courts of Foley Square.

Turning to the east, the approaches of the Brooklyn Bridge—Manhattan's grand architectural achievement of 1883—are visible. They are roadways to a structure that made the creation of the City of Greater New York inevitable. And finally, as the circle is completed, modern stores and Pace University, located where *The New York Times* once had its headquarters, appear. Almost all of Manhattan's newspapers were found on Park ("Newspaper") Row in the nineteenth century.

Modern Manhattan has dozens of distinct neighborhoods, but just beyond the modern Civic Center lie several of the most historically memorable ones. Contemporary Chinatown occupies many blocks behind the courts complex and covers the same streets that once held the nineteenth century's most notorious slum—the Irish Five Points district. In 1842, Charles Dickens concluded that "all that is loathsome, drooping and decayed" was found there, and when presidential candidate Abraham Lincoln visited Five Points in 1860, he needed a ten-man police escort.

Ultimately the Irish moved on, and part of the area was incorporated into Little Italy, where Italian immigrants colonized the blocks by area and dialect as if to replicate their former nation. On the adjacent Lower East Side, Jewish arrivals crowded into tenements to create the greatest population densities in world history. Separating those areas today is the fabled Bowery. Although the old song may say that, "we never go there any more," many New Yorkers still do, as eastern parts of Manhattan undergo gentrification. It is also worth noting that present-day housing projects along the East River occupy some of Governor Peter Stuyvesant's seventeenth-century farmland.

Above City Hall are found modern neighborhoods that figure prominently in the social and art world. Tribeca, short for "triangle below Canal Street," was once the "butter and eggs" purveyor to the city—home to warehouses and the Washington Market. Renovations that began in the 1980s have totally altered this area's image. It now features some of the priciest lofts and most expensive restaurants in Manhattan. One intersection in Tribeca honors the memory of architect James Bogardus, whose cast iron buildings fill these sections of Manhattan. The huge loft spaces with natural light found in neighboring SoHo (South of Houston Street) made it a destination for artists such as Romare Bearden, Claes Oldenberg, Yoko Ono, and Red Grooms in the 1960s. The rentable spaces in these two downtown neighborhoods made them "hot" for a generation of speculation and growth. Manhattan is an ever-changing city, but its ability to reuse the world's largest concentration of cast iron buildings showed extraordinary ingenuity. By the year 2000, rising prices were forcing aspiring artists to leave locales they had once avidly sought.

In their unending campaign to attract new customers, real estate agents constantly tout new areas. NoHo, the area "North of Houston Street," and Nolita, the district "North of Little Italy," are two of their recent creations. But no agent needs to inform buyers of the enduring charm to be discovered in Greenwich Village, Washington Square, and the East Village. Stretching below 14th Street between the rivers, these neighborhoods began as suburbs where elite New Yorkers could escape the population press of lower Manhattan. Their streets are filled with history, from the Cooper Union, where Lincoln came to warn of civil war, to Hester Street, where Jewish peddlers began to learn American business. The ambiance of these almost mythic locations in city history, home to both bohemians and bourgeoisie, is captured in part by postcards, which convey the continuing pleasures of lower Manhattan. ✒

Active river traffic and skyscrapers together convey a sense of Manhattan's allure. [c.1950]

FEDERAL COURT AND SUPREME COURT BUILDINGS, NEW YORK CITY 21

Municipal Building, New York.

Lower Manhattan is the center of both the judicial and administrative heartbeats of civic life. At left are the courthouses at Foley Square. [c.1940] The card at right shows the Municipal Building at City Hall Park. [c.1917]

At the turn of the century, Manhattan had dozens of newspapers. A half dozen leading dailies were located on Newspaper Row, east of City Hall. By 2000, the metropolis was reduced to only four major papers, yet still more than any other American city. [c.1897]

Saint Paul's Chapel, New York.

E-1213 Post Office, New York.

Manhattan's unique ability to happily reconcile all types of architecture was evident near City Hall. At left is Saint Paul's Chapel, perhaps the city's most ancient public building. [c.1911] Saint Paul's easily coexisted with both Park Row skyscrapers and unique structures like the French Second Empire-style Post Office (right) [c.1914], which was razed in 1938.

The bustle of lower Manhattan is evident in this early twentieth-century postcard, which shows the exodus of people from the Brooklyn Bridge into City Hall Park. The mayor, courts, central post office, and newspaper offices were centered here until the focus of business moved to Midtown. [c.1906]

Crossing the Brooklyn Bridge

As nineteenth-century Manhattan continued its slow march northward, civic boosters, dreaming of a greater city, schemed to unite with Brooklyn—America's fourth-largest city. The two rivals were separated by the swift currents of the East River, and ferry service between them was often disrupted. A bridge was the obvious solution. Modern New York has over 2,000 bridges; seventy-six are over waterways, but none captures the heart and imagination as completely as the Brooklyn Bridge. Its construction is one of engineering's greatest accomplishments.

Engineer John Roebling, the inventor of steel wire cable, believed that he could construct a bridge twice as long as any in existence across a wild river with a questionable bottom. Brooklyn politicians led by Henry C. Murphy endorsed that dream and achieved incorporation for the New York Bridge Company in April 1867. After a tragic accident killed Roebling before construction began, his son, Washington, a Civil War hero, replaced him as engineer and architect. Washington designed the caisson system that was essential for construction of twin bridge towers, the tallest structures in the United States when completed in 1877.

Washington fell victim to the bends in 1872 after he supervised work on the western caisson, a tower that still rests on questionable soil. He would be an invalid for the rest of his life, yet he still controlled bridge construction with the aid of a telescope and on-site direction by Emily, his extraordinary wife. After the towers were completed, it took another seven years to accomplish the Herculean task of creating and stringing fourteen miles of wire cable, which spanned 1,595 feet over the East River.

President Chester A. Arthur dedicated the Brooklyn Bridge on May 24, 1883, thirteen years after construction began. Its cost was $16 million, only a third of which came from Manhattan, but its completion made certain the creation of the City of Greater New York in 1898. Four other bridges would soon connect Manhattan to Long Island (Brooklyn and Queens Counties), but none would have the impact of what is probably the world's most famous bridge. The Brooklyn Bridge is an icon of both the city it serves and the nation it honors.

Architectural critic Lewis Mumford called the Brooklyn Bridge "perhaps the most completely satisfying structure" in the United States. It is truly the "eighth wonder of the world." [c.1913]

Tammany Hall and the Tweed Courthouse

Tammany Hall, the political machine that dominated New York City for a century after 1865, was originally formed as a social club in 1788. The Society of Saint Tammany relied on American Indian insignia and ceremonies to attract members, who soon became part of the Democratic Party. This organization transformed immigrants into voters, opposed nativism, and fought for wider suffrage and worker protection laws.

The "wigwam" of Tammany's "braves" on 14th Street was the center of political life in Manhattan from 1868 to 1929. Many "sachems" became wealthy from "honest graft." [c.1910]

As Manhattan's population became half foreign born, Tammany's power steadily increased, and after 1860, William Marcy Tweed was its first leader recognized as "Boss." Tweed organized a "Ring" of confederates and together they presided over a notoriously corrupt chapter in Manhattan's political history.

Manhattan's most enduring vestige of Tweed's regime is the elegant courthouse at 52 Chambers Street immediately north of City Hall. Building appropriations of $350,000 were authorized in 1858, but responsibility for completing the job fell to the Ring after the Civil War. The "house that Tweed built" became a monument to fraud and creative accounting. Annual postwar appropriations far exceeded the building's projected costs as a system of kickbacks (35 percent for contractors, 25 percent for Tweed, 40 percent for the rest of the Ring) was established. Marble for the courthouse came from Tweed's own quarry; carpeting yardage could have covered City Hall Park twice over; and the delivery of three tables and forty chairs cost $179,729. Bills submitted by Philip Dummy and T.C. Cash were promptly paid, while no fewer than five dead men served as janitors. Tweed and his Ring were displaced in the 1870s, but for years, lawsuits plagued a courthouse that cost at least $13 million to complete. In a final humiliation, the structure needed another $2 million in "repairs" before its formal opening in 1880.

Despite its lurid history, the Tweed Courthouse is a magnificent building. It provided Manhattan with decades of service as a city and county court, and later as office and archival space. Modern preservationists documented its unique qualities, and in 1996, Republican Mayor Rudolph Giuliani ordered its $35 million restoration. In an echo of Tweed, costs more than doubled to $89 million before the project was completed. Tammany's fabled wigwam on 14th Street is long vanished, but the Tweed Courthouse is a treasure of Manhattan and an outstanding example of nineteenth-century craftsmanship.

SINGER BUILDING, NEW YORK,

TALLEST BUILDING
IN THE WORLD
(42 STORIES, 638 FEET HIGH)

From 1908 to 1909, the Singer Building (left), distinctively clad in red brick and bluestone, was the tallest skyscraper in Manhattan. When razed in 1967, it was the largest structure ever demolished. [c.1908]

The Woolworth Building (right) on City Hall Park reigned as the world's tallest from 1913 to 1929. [c.1917]

Life in Greenwich Village

The huge section of lower Manhattan stretching north from Houston (pronounced HOW-ston) to 14th Street, and from the Hudson River to Broadway, is the "spiritual zone of mind" known as Greenwich Village. One of the oldest Manhattan communities and notorious for its difficult geography (4th Street crosses 12th Street), "the Village" has always been identified with lifestyles seeking freedom from restrictions.

Originally swampy woodland, the area was transformed into valuable fertile fields by hard-working Dutch farmers. Not until 1713 did English maps label it Grin'wich after the Thames port, and by 1800, it held both large estates and small plots that were cultivated by free blacks. The Village was so far north of Manhattan's populated area that a potter's field and prison were located there. Its landholders, however, were influential enough to win exemption from the pattern of grid blocks imposed in 1811, so the area retained its isolation and meandering lanes. The enduring charm of the Village's unusual street layout would draw artists, poets, tourists, and millionaires there for the next two centuries.

The cool breezes of the Hudson provided the Village with a reputation for having a healthy environment, and wealthy city residents of the nineteenth-century city used it as their refuge from fever, typhus, and cholera epidemics. The Erie Canal, completed in 1825, brought immigrant laborers to docks along the Hudson, and the area's population quadrupled between 1820 and 1850. But more affluent residents stayed in the center of the island, and fine row housing was constructed around Washington Square. To fill their needs, cultural institutions such as New York University and the Astor Library were created, and their conservative voting patterns won a nickname for the Village—the Empire Ward.

On the western edge of the Village, trade flourished and manufacturing gradually dominated the area. As more immigrants arrived, once fine buildings were subdivided and tenements constructed. The wealthier Villagers followed the city north, and Greenwich Village became a low-rent, ethnically diversified backwater that welcomed impoverished blacks and Italians, fiery European socialists, food mongers of every sort, and a number of poets and artists. Novelist Herman Melville oversaw customs collections on its docks for decades,

Is it an Old Master? The work of a young apprentice? Will it fit by the chair? Will you take $30? [c.1946]

◀ (Opposite) Originally the "American ward" of growing Manhattan, Greenwich Village was bypassed by the expanding city and became a center for bohemian lifestyles early in the twentieth century. Today, it is characterized by upscale living, but echoes of its past emerge at every village art show. [c.1962]

and poet Hart Crane wrote of the "headlights" of sin he observed in streets dominated by figures such as Ada Clare, "Queen of Bohemia."

Bypassed by the expanding city, Greenwich Village permitted each individual to define normality. Artists turned slums into studios and workshops, and in 1913, with the patronage of heiress Mabel Dodge Luhan, were able to put together the Armory Show—the first presentation of post-impressionist art in the United States. It was quite a significant event. "New women" such as Louise Bryant and Edna Saint Vincent Millay preached sexual revolution, while publications like *New Masses* and activists such as Emma Goldman called for political change. Eugene O'Neill drank at the Golden Swan, where he found characters for *The Iceman Cometh;* his plays appeared at the Provincetown Playhouse on MacDougall Street. Early American writers as varied as Edgar Allan Poe, Henry James, Mark Twain, and William Dean Howells found inspiration in the Village, and over the years, the literary procession was extended to include authors Thomas Wolfe, Willa Cather, John Dos Passos, and John O'Hara.

The Interborough Rapid Transit (IRT) subway came to the Village in 1918, and by the 1920s, the area's inaccessibility was ended. Yet the Village remained a separate state of mind. During Prohibition, drink was always available there. Around Sheridan Square alone, speakeasies such as the Black Parrot, the Blue Horse, the Green Witch, and the Vermillion Hound offered illegal spirits. Their presence drew many tourists, who were viewed as "bourgeois contamination" by many radicals. Thus, even before the Holland Tunnel's completion in 1927, the left-wing exodus had begun.

As America experienced the Depression and a series of wars, the once lurid reputation of the Village moderated; it became as much a tourist attraction as a haven for the nonconformist. Art galleries, coffee houses, and restaurants proliferated; clubs such as the Village Vanguard made jazz the unofficial music of the area; and the "new journalism" of the *Village Voice,* which premiered in 1955, took on municipal corruption as well as uptown pretension. The generation of Beat poets came and vanished, and the large gay community, which had always found sanctuary in the Village, established its legitimacy. A 1969 police raid at the Stonewall Inn is credited with launching the gay rights movement.

The Village became a center of political clout. The community defeated a Robert Moses Expressway project, protested against the Vietnam War, fought for AIDS services, and filed environmental briefs that sank the Westway road development. After the Landmarks Commission designated over 2,000 Village buildings as a historic district in 1969, the guarantee of developmental stability brought many more affluent residents into the area.

Today, the Village is both gentrified and alluring, and only sections such as Gansevoort Street, where meat cutters still openly practice their trade, recall a more earthy history. Annual parades on Halloween and Gay Pride Day are reminders of its more colorful past.

who's no lady?

Although enveloped by Manhattan in the 1850s, Greenwich Village remained apart due to its artists and writers. A hint of its colorful character is found in attractions such as the "femme impersonators" of the 82 Club. [c.1971]

Washington Square

As immigrants crowded into the warrens of the East Side, New Yorkers of the upper classes sought to escape the bustle of lower Manhattan and the dangerous precincts along both riverfronts. The land that became Washington Square had been used as a potter's field for Manhattan from 1797 to the 1820s, doubling as an execution site. When officials designated it as a military parade ground, marchers discovered that cannons sank into the unstable ground. Finally, the area became a public square.

Following the British practice of building homes around a park, developers began erecting brick residences along the park's south side. By 1831, a more elegant row of homes was completed on the north side. Many wealthy people, seeking greater gentility, moved north from the Bowery and into these houses. By 1840, a fountain flowed in the center of Washington Square's promenade area. New York University first occupied the park's eastern fringes before dominating the area in the twentieth century. In 1911, one of New York's greatest tragedies, the Triangle Shirtwaist fire, in which 146 young girls died, occurred only a block from the Square.

The most distinctive feature of today's Washington Square is its magnificent arch. In 1889, Manhattan celebrated the centenary of George Washington's inauguration by erecting several memorial arches, including one designed by Stanford White. Reminiscent of Paris's Arc de Triomphe, White's wooden ivory-painted monument was placed about 100 feet from the square's north side at the start of Fifth Avenue, and illuminated with electric lights. It was such a success that a 70-foot tall permanent structure won approval and community funding. As White's marble arch went up, so did his Judson Memorial Church on the southern edge of the square. Featuring sculptures by Frederick MacMonnies, the Washington Square Memorial Arch was dedicated on May 4, 1895, and has been an icon of the city ever since. In 1917, the arch was occupied by young radicals led by John Sloan, who proclaimed the formation of the Free and Independent Republic of Washington Square. Fortunately, they sobered up the next day, so the secession of Greenwich Village was rescinded.

Motor traffic ran through the arch until 1964, when the park was enclosed. It continues to play an important role in the life of the surrounding community.

Completed in 1895, the Washington Arch frames the entry to Fifth Avenue. Statues honoring Washington as a general and a president were added later. [c.1914]

Washington Arch, New York City.

Copyright 1905 by the Rotograph Co.

G 132a Cooper Union, N. Y. City.

Peter Cooper, an industrialist turned philanthropist, presented Cooper Union for the Advancement of Science and Art to Manhattan in 1859. Public events were held in its Great Hall, including an 1860 address by Abraham Lincoln. Gifted engineering students still receive a tuition-free education thanks to Cooper. [c.1905]

Lower Manhattan's Hester and Mulberry Streets convey images of ethnicity, poverty, and determination, and are integral to the success stories of immigrant Jews and Italians. [c.1908]

Hester Street, New-York.

507. NEW YORK STREET LIFE.
CHEESE VENDERS ON MULBERRY STREET

The Platinachrome Co. N.Y. Printed in America

Villages in the City

Lower Manhattan is not all civic glory; it also features neighborhoods settled since colonial times. Its interlaced streets were once prime farmland, *bouweries* producing food and tobacco for New Amsterdam. After the Revolution, as Manhattan expanded northward and immigrants crowded into the city, residential blocks were developed along both riverbanks, swampland and streams were filled in, and tenement housing was constructed for the waves of newcomers. Hard-working people built neighborhoods that gave intensity and drive to Manhattan. The Lower East Side accepted and tamed these successive surges of populations, becoming a "melting pot" for peoples and a cauldron of "memory culture."

Perhaps the first of Manhattan's ethnic enclaves was located from the Bowery to the East River, an area called *Kleindeutschland* or "Little Germany." Early in the nineteenth century, German immigrants congregated there by the thousands, living a close-knit existence that was free of the bustle of the lower city. Many were burghers rather than poor workers, and they would resent later arrivals with less means. Many practiced the German art of brewing, and some of these beer makers would later emigrate east to Brooklyn. Early in the twentieth century, other Germans moved northward to populate Yorkville in upper Manhattan.

In the early 1800s, immediately beyond the area where the Municipal Building now stands, was the Collect, a large freshwater pond on which John Fitch had tested a prototype steamboat in 1796. Its shoreline once provided picnic grounds for the residents of lower Manhattan. But this bucolic retreat became polluted as the slaughterhouses, tanneries, and breweries essential to a growing city expelled toxic waste into the pond. Therefore, when City Hall was being constructed, nearby hills were leveled and the Collect was filled in. The pond's northward flow towards the Hudson River became Canal Street, and the resulting land became part of Manhattan's Sixth Ward. This area, which remained spongy and prone to collapse, housed mostly poor Irish and free blacks. Rampant disease and harsh conditions were the rule here and its prime intersection, known as the Five Points, became notorious. Eventually, the tenements were razed and replaced by the court complex of what is now Foley Square. Pumps in the basements of these buildings constantly contend with

City legend claims that many fortunes began on the pushcarts of Mulberry Street, one of Manhattan's most crowded areas. [c.1907]

East of the Bowery and south of Houston Street was the ▶
"Jewish ghetto," perhaps the most mythical area of
Manhattan. Thousands of prominent Americans claim
their roots are found on its crowded streets. [c.1911]

still-flowing underground streams—modern reminders of the nineteenth-century Collect and the Five Points.

Ethnic succession has often been the rule of Manhattan life, and in time, the Irish moved up in the city hierarchy to serve as policemen, firemen, and judges. By 1890, newly immigrated Italians came to dominate the streets east of Broadway. They created the newspaper *Il Progresso* in 1880 and founded Our Lady of Pompeii parish in 1892. The area, which came to be known as Little Italy, first celebrated the Feast of San Gennaro in 1926. All of Manhattan now shares in this joyous annual street festival.

Farther to the east, Jewish immigrants lived a much-chronicled and almost romanticized life on many of the streets that had once been Kleindeutschland. The commercial bustle of Rivington and Hester Streets, and the wonder of having over 300 synagogues within a mile-wide area played vital roles in the saga of the Jewish Ghetto. The neighborhood's Public School 20 alone graduated George and Ira Gershwin, Edward G. Robinson, George Burns, and Louis Lefkowitz, while Eddie Cantor first sang in the choir of the Eldridge Street Synagogue, now a city landmark.

In 1900, half a million Jews lived on the Lower East Side, but their successful adaptation to American life reduced that number to only 20,000 by 1980. When New York built the Williamsburg Bridge over the East River in 1903, it became known as the "Jewish highway" out of the East Side. In spite of the recent influx of a large Orthodox population near Second Avenue—once called "Jewish Broadway"—lower Manhattan displays only vestiges of the huge Italian and Jewish communities of its past. It is worth remembering, however, that two-thirds of the city, over a million people, lived in East Side tenements in 1890, an era that is somewhat recaptured at the Tenement Museum on Orchard Street.

Since the "Chinese Mayflower" arrived in New York in 1847, there has been a growing Asian presence in Manhattan. In 1900, approximately 6,000 Chinese workers—a "bachelor society" comprised mostly of men—clustered onto a few blocks north of Chatham Square. By the year 2000, Manhattan's Asian population numbered over 100,000 and constituted the largest Chinatown in the Western Hemisphere. Chinatown continues to be one of the most mysterious enclaves within the city. In its streets, Sun Yat-sen raised money for revolution, tong wars were fought, garment industry sweatshops continue to mock labor laws, and ABCs (American Born Chinese) compete for power with those labeled FOBs (Fresh Off the Boat).

Manhattan's reputation is often defined by tall buildings, financial institutions, advertising and retail establishments, and cultural wonders; but it is a far more complex organism. Amid the bustle of commerce and industry, a myriad of neighborhoods have offered stability and solace to residents for hundreds of years.

Saint Anthony of Padua and Our Lady of Pompeii parishes served Greenwich Village's Italian population. Street fairs in the area continue to be held, although the ethnicity of the neighborhood has changed. [c.1915]

Monday Morning in N. Y. City

Please — stop praying, if you don't, we will all be drowned.

Jack.

Monday wash was hung out to dry early in the morning. It had to be taken in before soot from restarted factories filled the air. Housewives in tenements prided themselves on keeping clean apartments and sending properly dressed children into the world. [c.1901]

Chinatown. New York City.

In the 1890s, Manhattan's Chinatown numbered only 3,000 people and covered barely three blocks. [c.1905]

GREETINGS FROM CHINATOWN, NEW YORK

Always self-contained and mysterious, Chinatown's ever-expanding area now covers two square miles, has almost engulfed Little Italy, and is the largest Asian community in the United States. [c.1932]

THE BOWERY, BY NIGHT, NEW YORK

The Bowery was Manhattan's theater district until city population moved north, and the area fell into decline. Once the Third Avenue el train was removed in the 1950s, it began a slow gentrification process. [c.1907]

South Street Seaport

Manhattan's multiple relationships to the waters that surround it are demonstrated by the history of South Street—a center of commercial activity until well beyond the Civil War. Since colonial days, ships had avoided the high Hudson River shores and its prevailing north wind, opting instead for easier, more secure anchorages along the East River. Manhattan responded to the need for storage and commercial space by extending the shoreline through landfill. In 1811, merchant Peter Schermerhorn financed the construction of four-story warehouses on Fulton Street, which are now the oldest commercial buildings in the city. A public market for selling fish was added to the complex in 1821. By the 1840s, Walt Whitman lovingly described the seaport as a "forest of masts," and South Street became world famous.

By 1900, shallow East River moorings and deteriorating wharf facilities caused oceangoing shipping to transfer to the Hudson River and Brooklyn. South Street's Fulton Fish Market remained busy, and famed restaurants like Sweet's and Sloppy Louie's continued to serve happy patrons, but there was no question that South Street had deteriorated.

Blight characterized the area until citizens founded the Friends of South Street Maritime Museum. The museum, which opened in 1967, possesses one of the world's finest collections of historic ships, including the *Ambrose Lightship,* the three-masted *Wavertree,* and the four-masted *Peking.* To further maintain the area, preservationists prevented the destruction of Schermerhorn Row and other historic buildings, while waves of volunteers offered their time for rehabilitation efforts. Promises of state and city support led the Rouse Corporation to begin a commercial redevelopment, and in 1983, the opening of Fulton Market opposite the museum began luring people back into the area. Rehabilitated piers, art galleries, bars, and harbor tours, as well as unparalleled views of the East River and the Brooklyn Bridge, soon made the seaport a popular tourist destination and part of city nightlife.

The gentrification ultimately caused the Fulton Fish Market to move its operation to the Bronx, but under South Street's modern glitter, the alert visitor can still discern evidence of its vigorous past.

The East River wharves, a "forest of masts" centered about the "street of ships," have been vital to Manhattan's commerce for over two centuries. [c.1915]

Built to evoke memories of the recreation piers of the past, South Street's Pier 17 is filled with galleries, boutiques, and restaurants. It offers views of modern river traffic and glimpses into past history. [c.1988]

Williamsburg Bridge Approach,
New York City.

The Williamsburg Bridge

Increasingly intolerable traffic conditions on the Brooklyn Bridge prompted the creation of a second great span to cross the East River. Construction of the Williamsburg Bridge began in 1896 and was completed in 1903. It was the world's longest and heaviest suspension bridge, a complex stretching 7,308 feet.

Often referred to as the "Jewish highway" out of Manhattan, it provided a route from Delancey Street on Manhattan's crowded Lower East Side to Williamsburg, Brooklyn. The exodus shifted the center of population density from Manhattan to Williamsburg by 1917. After closing for repairs in 1988, the Williamsburg Bridge resumed its function as a city workhorse. Strolling across its pedestrian walkway remains a stirring city experience.

Eating and shopping are still major activities along Delancey Street, located on the Manhattan side of the Williamsburg Bridge. But the days of a "nickel a pickle" are long gone. [c.1910]

Brooklyn and Manhattan Bridges, New York.

The Manhattan Bridge—the third lower-East River crossing—opened for traffic in December 1909. The least inspiring of the city's suspension bridges, its flawed design had trains rumbling across its edges, rather than along the inside, causing severe sway. Repair costs were twenty times the original cost of the bridge. [c.1912]

CHAPTER THREE
*M*idtown Manhattan

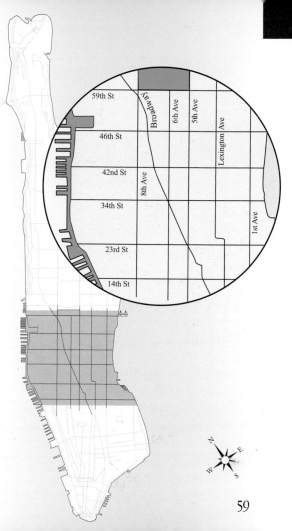

*I*n 1811, New York adopted a plan for the future development of Manhattan Island, a long-range vision of systematic expansion that seemed overly optimistic for a city whose population was still centered below City Hall. Totally indifferent to the topography of upper Manhattan, the Commissioner's Plan mandated that a rectangular grid created by 12 avenues and 155 cross streets would regularize the future metropolis. This layout would be somewhat altered, most prominently by Broadway—the long diagonal street that slashed across the city—and by the creation of Central Park; but basically, this simple scheme would largely determine the way in which Manhattan grew. In stark contrast to the crazy quilt of downtown neighborhoods, the streets of Midtown (14th Street to 59th Street) demonstrate order and domination over nature itself. They permit the sun to light them in the east, open river views to the west, and offer a scheme guaranteeing easy pedestrian navigation.

The uniformity of Midtown Manhattan houses the workings of America's capitalistic machinery. Financiers may look to Wall Street and ethnicity may thrive in the neighborhoods above City Hall, but twentieth-century Midtown is where the action takes place. Here, Manhattan's obsession with money becomes palpable; the real estate of its streets and massive buildings is the most expensive on earth. But oddly enough, this golden enclave is approached through a series of neighborhoods that retain much of their nineteenth-century origins.

The gateway from lower Manhattan to the wonders of Midtown passes through Union Square, one of several gathering places that forged the development of the area. Called Union Place under the Commissioner's Plan, the intersection where Broadway and the Bowery come together has been called Union Square since 1831; it honors neither the heroism of the Civil War era nor the legions of workingmen who later rallied within its precincts. During the nineteenth century, it was filled with residences, theaters such as the Academy of Music, and shops such as Tiffany & Co. Until the 1970s, middle-class shoppers patronized area department stores, including Klein's on the Square, Hearn's, and Mays, while art lovers could visit Andy Warhol's "factory," perhaps in search of "fifteen minutes of fame." Changing retail patterns and the rise of a drug culture led to area decline only reversed in the 1990s. Today's Union Square features renovated statuary, community playgrounds, a popular greenmarket, and modern structures like Zeckendorf Tower.

Skaters at Rockefeller Center

Distinct neighborhoods spread out across Manhattan from Union Square to play their roles in the modern city. East from the Square are the huge residential complexes of Stuyvesant Town and Peter Cooper Village, while Gramercy Park and Murray Hill to its north retain a gentility reminiscent of earlier times. To the west of the Square, Chelsea dates back to the 1750s when it was farmland. After 1813, it became the estate of Clement Clarke Moore, who gave the world "A Visit From Saint Nicholas." At first, Moore resented the advance of Manhattan's expanding street grid, but ultimately he became a land developer and philanthropist. His generosity created both a theological seminary and Saint Peter's Church in 1838.

Chelsea's streets later became part of the Ladies Mile shopping area, held a nineteenth-century theater district, played home to several early movie studios, and hosted Manhattan's first public housing project in 1946. Manhattan's flower district has long been centered in Chelsea, and although the construction of high-rise apartments and art galleries has recently changed this neighborhood's population mix, its vibrancy has not been dimmed. At the Chelsea pier, long decaying Hudson River docks have been renovated to recapture Manhattan's waterfront heritage. Less successful were similar plans for Hell's Kitchen—the storied Irish enclave located north of Chelsea that was once notorious for its gangs. Yet Midtown land is so valuable that the process of gentrification has recently engulfed Hell's Kitchen, whose residents now call it Clinton.

Manhattan, when viewed from either of its rivers, offers the appearance of a valley. The towers of the Financial District slope down into miles of neighborhoods before Midtown's towers again rise skyward. Within the space of a Midtown mile are found dozens of the world's most famous skyscrapers, among them the Empire State, Chrysler, MetLife, and Citicorp buildings, as well as the unrivaled office complex of Rockefeller Center. Midtown offers the most impressive civic architecture, including Grand Central Terminal, the New York Public Library, and the United Nations, as well as Manhattan's most visited public venues, such as the Jacob Javits Center, Herald Square, and Madison Square Garden.

Midtown Manhattan's most famous neighborhood is Times Square—"the Crossroads of the World." Since 1904, the intersection of Broadway and 42nd Street has been the center of New York's entertainment industry and an obligatory tourist destination. Times Square means New Year's Eve, bright lights (which have evolved from candles, to gas, electric, neon, and today's digital marvels), and the finest theatrical productions on earth. Tourists arrive by the millions, and recent efforts to remove grime and sleaze have been entirely successful. More family oriented than ever before, contemporary Times Square is simply the most vital part of Manhattan, an area that belongs to the world as much as New York.

Every Midtown block suggests the power of the city. It boasts some of the finest hotels, the priciest boutiques, and the most exclusive restaurants in the world. It contains Madison Avenue, the nation's advertising capital; Park Avenue, its international business heart; the world-renowned Garment Center on Seventh Avenue. One of the world's most famous streets for shopping is Fifth Avenue, while cultural treasures such as the Museum of Modern Art and Carnegie Hall are known for drawing discriminating crowds. No one is surprised to learn that Midtown contains more lawyers than any other place in the world. It is quite simply the most vital part of the most vital city on earth. ❧

Radio City Music Hall—home of the world-famous Rockettes—has entertained millions of visitors since December 1932. [c.1962]

Rockefeller Center is the "American acropolis," the largest commercial building project in national history. No postcard can fully display its wonders, which include rooftop terraces, ice skating under the gaze of Prometheus, and Radio City performances. [c.1949]

Union Square,
New York City.

Union Place was a popular promenade site even before its designation as a square in 1831. It was the hotel and shopping center of Manhattan in the nineteenth century, declined in the twentieth, and experienced a renovation in the 1990s that again drew crowds to the area. [c.1922]

MACY'S DEPARTMENT STORE AND HERALD SQUARE. NEW YORK.

At the turn of the twentieth century, the Sixth Avenue elevated train and several trolley lines brought shoppers to Herald Square, where the Straus brothers had relocated their department store in 1902. [c.1907]

Shopping in Manhattan

Every city boasts of its commercial areas, but no metropolis is identified more with the art of retailing than New York. From its earliest fur traders to the creators of dry goods empires to the high-class boutiques and jewelry centers of Fifth Avenue, Manhattan has always established the nation's sense of fashion and satisfied the desires of the buying public. Although every city neighborhood has its special shopping area, particular segments of Midtown's unending commercial stream merit further consideration.

After 200 years of uninhibited individual enterprise, Manhattan gave birth to the department store. Perhaps fittingly, the man responsible for this commercial revolution was an Irish immigrant, a Trinity College graduate named Alexander Turney Stewart. Ambitious and innovative, Stewart transformed his initial 500£ investment in Irish lace into a lavish eight-story "Marble Palace" on lower Broadway in 1846. Named for its founder, Stewart's was an establishment that featured large display windows and brought specialty stores under its roof as separate departments. As the population gradually moved north, so did Stewart, and his "Iron Palace" opened on Broadway and 10th Street in 1862. It was the first Manhattan building with a cast iron façade. Retail success made Stewart one of the richest men in Manhattan. His restless nature led him to create a model community in Garden City, Long Island, as well as build one of the earliest mansions on Fifth Avenue.

The marketing revolution that Stewart began led to the development of the "Ladies Mile." Running from 8th Street to 23rd Street, and Broadway to Sixth Avenue, this area was shopping "heaven" by the late nineteenth century. Whether the ladies came by carriage, walked, or took the elevated "el" train, which began running in 1878, they knew that their personal needs and everything for their Victorian homes was available there. Among the famous shops were Arnold Constable, B. Altman's, Best & Co., Erlich's, Lord & Taylor, Macy's, Siegel-Cooper, W.&J. Sloane, and Wanamaker's, but dozens of other shops competed for consumer attention. A popular ditty of the time summarized the frantic shopping scene: *"From 8th Street down the men are making it, From 8th Street up the women are spending it. That is the manner of this great town, From 8th Street up and 8th Street down."* Far into the twentieth century, Ladies Mile was a shopping mecca, drawing

After 1900, the "Ladies Mile" moved east along 23rd Street towards the Flatiron Building. Within another decade, Herald Square and Fifth Avenue assumed the lead in Manhattan's shopping experience. [c. 1905]

Shopping in Manhattan

thousands of customers daily. Many of the sculptured cast iron fronts of its emporia still exist. In 1989, the Landmarks Commission designated a historic district of more than 400 buildings to recall its merchandising glory.

Rowland H. Macy, founder of Macy's dry goods shop, was responsible for several retailing firsts, such as staying open until midnight. After 1888, when ownership of the store was held by the Straus brothers, the inexorable northward shift of Manhattan's population encouraged the most enterprising merchants to move their base of operations. In 1902, the brothers made the daring decision to transfer retail operations uptown to a building on Herald Square on 34th Street. Isidor Straus died on the *Titanic* in 1912, but brother Nathan continued to run Macy's until 1925, making it a national chain. In 1927, Macy's organized its first Thanksgiving Day Parade, now a national TV extravaganza. In time, the "world's largest store" would fill an entire city block and set the standard for department stores everywhere.

For decades, Macy's competed with Gimbel's and B. Altman's, retailers who had moved north. Each store offered its own brand-name items and hosted boutique counters within its walls. Gimbel's sought the same customers as Macy's, but Altman's adopted a more elegant and conservative style in its Fifth Avenue building. It featured thirty-nine elevators that were located around a central atrium, paneled rooms taken from Benjamin Altman's mansion, and a dedicated sales staff. Changing commercial trends ultimately closed Macy's long-time rivals in the 1980s, but

today, Altman's landmark building houses a division of the New York Public Library, the Graduate School of City University, and the Oxford University Press.

When Altman's opened, it was the only commercial center amid a bevy of fine residences, but as decades passed and Manhattan changed, 34th Street became the southern end of the world's most envied shopping district. Fifth Avenue up to 59th Street soon boasted a variety of department stores and specialty shops, and a host of jewelers. These merchants catered to discriminating consumers, refused to allow garish signs, and emphasized elegance of service; cost was rarely mentioned. Although many changes have occurred over time (establishments like Arnold Constable, Best & Co., and Bonwit Teller no longer exist), the presence of Tiffany & Co., Cartier, Bergdorf Goodman, and Saks Fifth Avenue continue to provide links to a shopping tradition that is uniquely Manhattan. And one must never forget Bloomingdale's, a department store with no downtown heritage that opened on Third Avenue and 59th Street in 1872; its "little brown bag" epitomizes the eternal quest of the ardent consumer.

Mention must also be made of the Woolworth lunch counter, the A&P supermarket, Hellman's mayonnaise, and the Oreo cookie, all of which were born in Manhattan. But even without such support, the point is clear. Whatever you seek to buy can be found in Manhattan, in greater variety and at a better price than anywhere else.

Originally a Philadelphia retailer, John Wanamaker purchased Alexander T. Stewart's Iron Palace in 1896, and by 1903 was one of Manhattan's leading retailers. This cast iron gem of a building was destroyed by fire in 1956. [c.1903]

7441   THE WANAMAKER STORE, NEW YORK.

The Flatiron Building

Located on a narrow triangle of land at the intersection of 23rd Street, Fifth Avenue, and Broadway, the Flatiron Building was never the tallest office tower in Manhattan, but it has always been one of its most beloved. Just after the turn of the century, a syndicate led by George Fuller hired architect Daniel Burnham, whose reputation was made at the Chicago Exposition of 1893, to create a useful commercial space on a challenging site. Structural engineer Corydon Purdy solved vexing wind-bracing problems, and Burnham designed a French Renaissance tower without setbacks. Their remarkable accomplishment opened in 1903 and has given joy to viewers ever since.

Originally called the Fuller Building, the structure is only six feet wide at its apex, and thrusts itself uptown like the prow of a ship; it seems unnaturally light and almost without volume. Winds continually buffet the corner, and the constant downdrafts have been known to lift women's skirts and blow unfortunate bike-riding messengers into traffic. Noted photographers like Edward Steichen and Alfred Stieglitz found the building an inspiration. From the moment the building was erected, viewers insisted that it should have been called "flatiron" because of its shape, rather than the Fuller Building. And when the Fuller Corporation moved out in 1929 to a more prestigious uptown location, the Manhattanites got their way.

The Flatiron Building still watches over the 6.2 acres of refurbished Madison Square Park. Elegant restaurants have combined with the nightlife and gallery scene of Chelsea to stimulate area revival. Whether seen in sunlight, mist, rain, or snow, the Flatiron Building is a vibrant symbol of Manhattan, one of its most photographed structures—a true American icon.

The wind-tunnel effect of the Fuller (Flatiron) Building drew crowds of onlookers, who were eager to watch pedestrians trying to cope with the constant downdrafts. [c.1905]

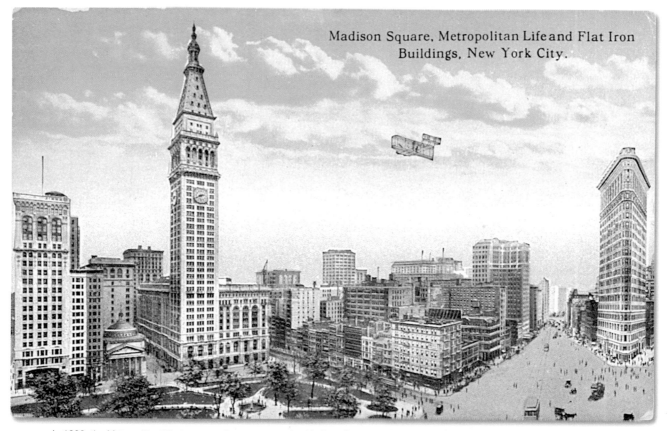

Madison Square, Metropolitan Life and Flat Iron Buildings, New York City.

In 1893, the Metropolitan Life Insurance Company moved to Madison Square, and by 1910 was the world's largest insurer. The MetLife Tower, built between 1906 and 1909, briefly reigned as the world's tallest building. Its famed four-faced clock still works. [c.1918]

Garden on the Move

For half of the nineteenth century, Madison Square, from 23rd to 26th Street, was located at the northern fringe of the city; it was home to a military barracks and a potter's field. In 1847, it was reshaped into a public park, named to honor a president, and became an entertainment center. The elegant Fifth Avenue Hotel and P.T. Barnum's Monster Classical and Geological Hippodrome opened on separate sides of the green in 1859. During the late 1870s, strollers on its paths were able to stop and admire the arm and torch of the Statue of Liberty, which was prominently displayed there for five years. Daily brass band concerts were held in the Hippodrome for several years before the building was altered and became the first Madison Square Garden in 1879.

In 1890, architect Stanford White redesigned the structure into the first American building totally devoted to entertainment. Covering the entire block from 26th to 27th Street and topped with a statue of Diana, the Garden's 304-foot Moorish tower promised pleasure. For thirty-five years, the Garden hosted events as varied as bike races, horse shows, Democratic Conventions, and concerts. In November of 1925, a third Garden opened at 8th Avenue and 50th Street. The new arena would host championship boxing matches as well as ice hockey games, rodeos, dog shows, and the circus. Mayor Jimmy Walker defended his reputation there before resigning, and college basketball's National Invitation Tournament began there in 1938. But the Garden's most golden moment may have been when Marilyn Monroe offered her rendition of "Happy Birthday" to President John F. Kennedy.

Physical inadequacies, such as limited seating and poor sight lines, forced the Garden to relocate again, and in 1968, Irving Feld spent $116 million to construct a circular arena on the two-block site above Pennsylvania Station. Manhattan was experiencing a real-estate boom, so its fourth Garden included a twenty-nine-floor office building. But for fans, it was primarily home to their beloved sports teams—the Rangers and Knicks.

Significant events at the present Garden include concerts by the Beatles and Frank Sinatra, prayer revivals led by the Reverend Billy Graham, two National Democratic Conventions, and a papal appearance. The addition of luxury boxes in 1992 made it clear that the Garden was a copious moneymaker, rather than just a place for fond memories. Whatever its future location, Madison Square Garden remains part of Midtown's legendary history.

Stanford White's distinctive Garden included a rooftop cabaret, where he was murdered by Henry Thaw in 1906. [c.1910]

Madison Square Garden, New York.
COPYRIGHT, 1910, BY IRVING UNDERHILL, N.Y.

Manhattan's fourth Madison Square Garden complex was constructed on the site above Penn Station.
The unending traffic of the world's busiest station surges below its arena. [c.1970]

The three highest Buildings in the World. New York.

Till 1906   1907   1908

Park Row Building
382 feet high.

Singer Building
593 feet high.

Metropolitan Life Building
48 Stories. 658 feet high.

Giants in the Metropolis

New York is a city of superlatives, most directly applied to Manhattan. It's a city of unique power, envied and loathed, respected and feared, mistrusted and misunderstood. Its scope and size overwhelm the national definition of what a city is, even as it establishes standards of incomparable achievement. Because bigness is integral to its definition, it seems inevitable that New York would perfect the skyscraper.

The skyscraper saga begins with the geologic foundation of Manhattan Island. The city rests on a unique formation of three rock layers that provide a solid foundation on which skyscrapers, regardless of the height they aspire to, can rise. Closest to the surface is renowned Manhattan schist, once the core of a vast mountain range that has worn down over eons and now constitutes the underlying bedrock of the island. The schist is closest to the surface at the tip of Manhattan and again in Midtown—locations where most of the modern-day skyscrapers rise.

Until the last years of the nineteenth century, the tallest structure in Manhattan was the 284-foot steeple of Trinity Church. But "sperm candle" construction in the 1850s showed a willingness to build higher, and the masonry bulks of the Equitable, Western Union, and Tribune buildings in the 1870s, demonstrated that broad and low neoclassic architecture no longer held sway. When owners discovered that renters would pay more for upper floors that were accessible by elevators, the future of skyscrapers became assured. The durability of the iron-framed Statue of Liberty proved that height could be achieved without massive concrete bases. Skyscrapers represented the most efficient use of space; they were "blocks turned on end" to house the armies of office workers needed to run modern businesses. Both insurance companies and corporations proved willing to finance tall headquarter buildings, which trumpeted their success. From 1890 to 1915, the modern New York skyline began to evolve.

Architectural history describes New York and Chicago locked in a struggle over which "invented" the skyscraper, but Manhattan clearly wins this historical battle. The Tower Building designed by Bradford Lee Gilbert used steel framing to rise eleven stories on a lot only 21.5 feet wide in 1889. Crowds first gathered in

The Times Tower opened in 1904 and has been the focus of Manhattan's New Year's Eve celebration ever since. [c.1907]

◀ (Opposite) Manhattan has always built upward toward the sky. When the Singer building was demolished in 1967, it was the largest structure ever razed. That designation ended when the World Trade Center fell in 2001. [c.1910]

anticipation of its fall, and then marveled at its ability to withstand the blizzard of 1888 and the hurricane of 1889.

Then in 1890, Joseph Pulitzer erected a "splendid pile" to house the offices of the *New York World*, a building topped by a golden dome that rose 309 feet. Visiting children asked, "Does God live here?," but a host of Pulitzer's rivals immediately planned new accommodations for other deities. According to architectural history, the Wall Street area alone held sixty-five skyscrapers before World War I. Elsewhere in Manhattan, notice must be given to the Times Tower, built in 1904 to a height of 362 feet; the 612-foot-tall Singer Building, erected in 1908; and the Metropolitan Life Insurance Building, built in 1910 at a height of 701 feet. The glorious 792-foot Woolworth Building reigned as the world's tallest structure for over a quarter of a century.

In 1916, New York adopted America's first zoning code—regulations designed to guarantee sunlight on streets below by mandating setbacks above. It took some years before builders mastered its requirements, but in time, Art Deco masterpieces like the Paramount and Chrysler Buildings were erected. The Empire State Building, constructed during the Depression, was the world's tallest building until 1973, and has become a familiar icon to moviegoers everywhere.

But the builders of Manhattan's skyscrapers have always been hardheaded businessmen. With land scarce, office space had to be maximized, and as long as interior services were adequate, exterior decorations could be minimal. Architectural simplicity guaranteed higher profits. In the 1950s, office buildings that were merely tall "glass boxes with flat roofs" dominated architectural drawing boards. Although the international style sometimes resulted in distinguished buildings, such as Lever House, built in 1952, or the Seagram Building, erected in 1957, more often, new structures merely filled sites to maximum height with minimal amenities. Contemporary Park Avenue offers an amazing vista, but not innovative architecture.

The tallest of all these "tall boxes" were the Twin Towers of the World Trade Center. Critics lamented their regularity, their bulk, and their lifeless plaza; but in time, these two buildings came to represent the enduring power and importance of the city. Hollywood paid the Towers their highest compliment by subjecting them to an attack by King Kong in the 1976 remake of the classic movie. Like Manhattan itself, they were symbols of American success.

Since the word "skyscraper" entered the American vocabulary in the 1890s, its primary context has been Manhattan, the island of high aspirations. Novelist Henry James saw their presence as evidence of "uncontested and unabashed pride," but skyscrapers are far more than vanity projects. They represent the most efficient use of scarce city space. They are urban monuments, indicative of both corporate wealth and the spirit of a city that constantly aspires to greatness. Manhattan's giants provide the city with the world's greatest skyline and a mystique that continues to attract the most adventurous and innovative minds on earth.

SKYSCRAPERS OF NEW YORK CITY

112

EMPIRE STATE BUILDING

RCA BUILDING IN ROCKEFELLER CENTER

CHRYSLER BUILDING

It was during the nation's worst economic depression that Manhattan unveiled three of its grandest structures, each providing evidence of the city's faith in the future. But economic forces were so powerful that for years, the Empire State Building was derided as the "Empty State" Building. [c. 1940]

2007 -- Metropolitan Opera House, New York.

Dear Lila This is where N.Y. 400 listens to Grand Opera with love to all Your Mother

Souvenir Post Card Co. New York and Berlin

The opening of the Metropolitan Opera House on Broadway between 39th and 40th Streets marked yet another northward leap in Manhattan's development. The new auditorium quickly replaced the Academy of Music on 14th Street as the center of operatic excellence. [c.1905]

5TH AVE., TRAFFIC SHOWING SIGNAL TOWER, NEW YORK

The elegant stores of Fifth Avenue have always drawn crowds of shoppers, and unceasing two-way traffic only compounded area congestion. In the years before traffic lights, policemen stationed in signal towers fought a losing battle against the tumult. [c.1931]

Times Square, New York City.   16

For over half a century, the Astor Hotel (at left) presided over Times Square—Midtown's entertainment center.
From 1941 to 1966, the Camel sign (at right) blew perfect smoke rings over the "Crossroads of the World." [c.1943]

Times Square at night is a festival of light, a shimmering wonderland that was dimmed only during World War II. It is an area in which advertisers enthusiastically compete for prime space. [c.1958]

The New Library, New York.

The New York Public Library is one of the world's premier research facilities. Designed by Carrère and Hastings, the Beaux Arts masterpiece opened in 1911, and today houses approximately 11 million items. [c.1913]

St. Patricks Cathedral, New York City.

Saint Patrick's Cathedral

Saint Patrick's Cathedral, the dream of Archbishop "Dagger John" Hughes, is home to the Archdiocese of New York and a famed New York site. James Renwich designed the cathedral, which replaced an earlier church on Prince Street, and its uptown location reflected Hughes' faith in Manhattan's future. Saint Patrick's does not rank among the world's ten largest churches but is among its most beloved. Critics suggest that its French Gothic style is less than ideal, but somehow the church seems perfectly at home among the skyscrapers, and it complements nearby Rockefeller Center. After twenty years of construction, the cathedral was dedicated on May 25, 1879 by John McCloskey, the first American cardinal.

James Renwich, the architect of Saint Patrick's Cathedral, also designed Grace Church and Saint Bartholomew's. [c.1913]

Rockefeller Center

Rockefeller Center is the most famous commercial development in American history, a complex of nineteen buildings extending over twenty-two acres in Midtown Manhattan. Often called "America's Acropolis," the project was originally intended to serve as home for a relocated Metropolitan Opera House, but the Crash of 1929 shattered that dream. Instead, John D. Rockefeller, Jr. ordered his architects to build a "commercial center as beautiful as possible," but one that could return profits. An army of 75,000 workers, laboring during the Depression, completed the first buildings by 1932, and also instituted the Christmas tree tradition. The annual lighting ceremony of a carefully selected fir is now an occasion shared by the entire country via television. By 1933, the centerpiece of the project—the RCA Building—had opened for business.

At the base of "30 Rock" sits a justly famous sunken plaza. Originally, this area was intended only as an entryway to underground shopping, but designers later transformed it into a summertime restaurant and a winter skating rink. As visitors amble down the sloping Channel Islands between the British and the French Buildings, they are greeted by a spectacular fountain where Paul Manship's "Prometheus" reigns; almost everyone takes a picture. At the top of the renamed General Electric Building is the Rainbow Room, which has been the most elegant of all Manhattan cabarets since 1934.

Ever since the 1940s, Rockefeller Center has been enormously profitable. Today it boasts ten landmark office buildings, including Associated Press and Time headquarters, as well as Radio City Music Hall. The nation was shocked when the complex was sold to the Mitsubishi Corporation in 1985, but after Japan's "Bubble Economy" burst, the Rockefellers repurchased it at a bargain price four years later. In December 2000, a real estate consortium purchased Rockefeller Center for $1.85 billion and ended the family connection with the nation's greatest monument to capitalistic enterprise.

The Waldorf Astoria Hotel, New-York.

Hotel Pennsylvania, New York City.

Luxury Hotels have always been essential to Manhattan's appeal. The first Waldorf-Astoria (left) was demolished so the Empire State Building could rlse on 34th Street. [c.1907] The Hotel Pennsylvania (right), immortalized by a Glenn Miller song, was built to provide accommodations for city visitors. [c.1923]

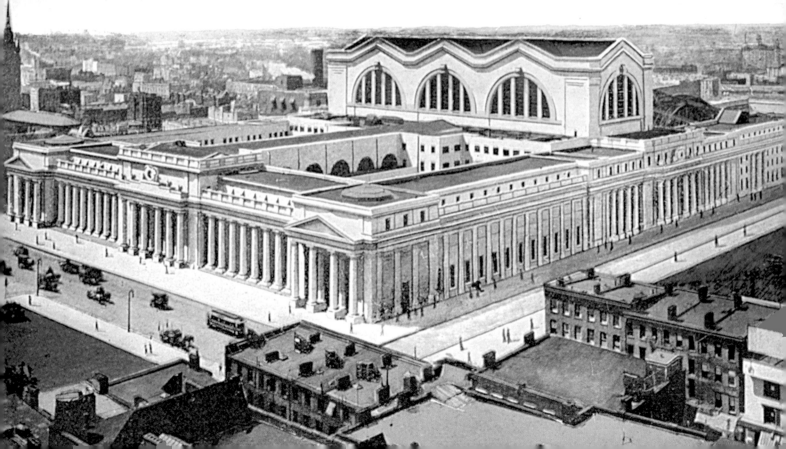

Bird's-eye View of the P. R. R. Depot, New York.

Transit Central

Getting around Manhattan has never been easy, but arguably, it was most convenient when New York was a "walking city." When merchants lived above their stores and trade and commerce were limited to the tip of the island, most laborers walked to work, so transportation was hardly a priority. As the economy expanded and Manhattanites began populating the grid of streets designed by the 1811 Commissioner's Plan, transit innovations became necessary. Eventually, the city would have an outstanding transit system headed by two of the world's finest railway stations.

In 1836, Manhattan was the first city to use the horse-drawn street railway. The New York and Harlem Railroad was the first of five horse-car lines, which carried 325 million fares by the time of the Civil War. A fleet of ferries brought additional workers from Brooklyn Heights to the Fulton Street docks. Yet, as the settled areas of Manhattan surged northward, neither ferry nor horse was adequate to meet commuting needs. A giant step forward came in 1868, when an elevated train line opened on Ninth Avenue. Belching steam and soot, engines soon made their way north along three parallel avenues—part of Manhattan's continuing battle to connect workers with their jobs.

Manhattan's ultimate people-mover was the subway, and when the city's first Interborough Rapid Transit (IRT) line opened in October 1904, the future had arrived. Only New York had the vision to create a four-track transit system, now covering 722 miles and offering around-the-clock local and express service in both directions. In the decades that followed, horses, ferries, and elevated trains would gradually vanish along with Manhattan's famed 5-cent fare, but the subway was always the best way to get around the city. New York, the "city that never sleeps," may find one cause of its insomnia in the clamor of its magnificent transportation system.

Seven decades of mobile innovation addressed the needs of city workers, but by 1900, Manhattan was also surrounded by expanding suburbs. Commuters in hundreds of trains needed better access to the dynamic center of the region. When the Pennsylvania Railroad, the nation's greatest carrier, purchased the Long Island Railroad in 1900, it also proposed to construct a single station in Manhattan to accept commuter streams to and

McKim, Mead and White's Penn Station was "vast enough to hold the sound of time." [c.1912]

◀ (Opposite) Opened in 1910, the original Pennsylvania Station, which was razed in the 1960s, was an architectural marvel. [c.1912]

Grand Central Station has been the hub of Midtown traffic ▶
since 1913. The construction of its circumferential elevated
roadway in 1919 was a successful attempt at eliminating
traffic jams. Renovated and rededicated in 1998, the
terminal services half a million passengers daily. [c.1919]

from the south, west, and east. In 1902, the city council endorsed the plan, and work on tunnels under both the Hudson and East Rivers accelerated.

Tunneling proceeded even as a new station designed by Charles McKim rose at Seventh Avenue and 32nd Street. Ultimately, eighty-four massive Doric columns, each thirty-five feet high, provided a magnificent entryway into Pennsylvania (Penn) Station. Admirers found the structure "vast enough to hold the sound of time." After opening on September 8, 1910, Penn Station served Manhattan commuters for fifty-two years, but its magnificence is now glimpsed only in photographs. Its demolition, which began in 1963, fostered preservation movements that have saved historic buildings in scores of American cities. Classic Penn Station was replaced by a remodeled, subterranean depot located beneath Madison Square Garden, an efficient terminal that ranks as the world's busiest.

Rail access to Manhattan from the north was totally controlled by the New York Central Railroad after 1869, and "Commodore" Cornelius Vanderbilt was determined to build a suitable depot for his trains. Grand Central Terminal on 42nd Street is the third structure to occupy the site, and from its opening in 1913 was hailed as America's "finest example of Beaux Arts civic planning." An elegant merger of form and function, the terminal featured the first duplex track system. It separated competing flows of long distance, commuter, subway, auto, and pedestrian traffic, and is considered one of the most beautiful structures in Manhattan. Its concourse is so large

that City Hall could easily fit inside, and pedestrians may contemplate the constellations on its blue ceiling if they can avoid being trampled. The monumental structure that was placed over its south-facing entry, entitled "Transportation," symbolized the vital role of railroads and commuters in the life of Manhattan. And unlike Pennsylvania Station, Grand Central Terminal fostered a construction boom in the surrounding streets, led to the creation of modern Park Avenue, and made Midtown around 42nd Street the heart of the twentieth-century metropolis.

By the 1960s, railroads were no longer profitable, so the New York Central corporation proposed to raze its terminal and erect a skyscraper in its place. Preservationists, who were outraged by the loss of the original Pennsylvania Station, united to oppose this atrocity and waged a bitter, decade-long legal battle. In 1978, the Supreme Court decided that the terminal must be saved. From 1995 to 1998, major renovations restored the station to its former glory, and the process stimulated yet another Midtown building boom.

Manhattan is world famous for its brutal traffic congestion, and Midtown is the center of its automobile nightmare. Pedestrians often make better time than taxis, buses, or cars, and wonder at the chaos in the streets. But if Manhattan has failed to meet the challenge of the automobile, its subways, railroads, and bridges still provide the metropolis with an unrivaled transportation web, and Midtown remains the heart of the entire system.

BILTMORE
HOTEL

125 PARK AVENUE SHOWING NEW YORK CENTRAL BUILDING.

NEW YORK CITY

3A-H105

The New York Central Building once towered over Park Avenue, as seen in the postcard at right. [c.1941] Known today as the Helmsley Building, it is overshadowed by international skyscrapers and the MetLife Building, as seen above.

A 168 Carnegie Music Hall and Lyceum, N. Y. City.

A chance meeting between conductor Walter Damrosch and philanthropist Andrew Carnegie led to the construction of Carnegie Hall in 1891.
Preservationists saved it from destruction in 1960, and you can still get there if you "practice, practice, practice." [c.1905]

United Nations

The East River site where the United Nations complex stands was once a jumble of run-down tenements, warehouses, and meat packers. The philanthropy of the Rockefeller family provided $8.5 million to purchase the property from a developer, and the City of New York appropriated $16 million, which allowed building czar Robert Moses to "bury" six blocks of First Avenue under the construction site. An international board of fifteen architects, headed by Wallace K. Harrison, created the spectacular design for the complex. In October 1952, the General Assembly moved into its new quarters. One of Manhattan's premier attractions for tourists, the United Nations confirms New York's position as "capital of the world."

From Queens, the view of the United Nations complex is one of New York's signature sights. [c.1966]

CHAPTER FOUR
The East Side

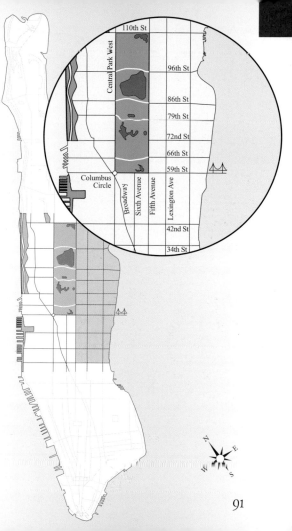

For most of the nineteenth century, the primary images conjured up by the words "East Side" were those of immigrant poverty, crowded tenements, and the incessant clamor raised by a population speaking different languages. But beyond the congestion of Manhattan's notorious ghetto, another world had always existed—a universe of great style, elegance, and affluence. From colonial times, the richest segment of Manhattan's population sought the vistas and the serenity of the East River shoreline. In the 1660s, Peter Stuyvesant established his farm and manor near the swift-running river; some 9,000 twentieth-century apartments were constructed in a nearby "town" that honors his memory. During the Federal Era, wealthy merchants such as Archibald Gracie built mansions situated to take advantage of East River breezes. Located in modern Carl Shurz Park, Gracie's home today serves as the official residence of the mayor of New York.

During its first two centuries, the bulk of Manhattan's population was densely packed below City Hall Park, while the East Side provided country living for the elite. In the modern city, the area above 34th Street retains a special aura of historic elegance. Quaker merchant Robert Murray selected a hilltop location for his new home in that area during the 1750s. City legend asserts that in 1776, his wife, Mary, entertained British General Sir William Howe so long at tea that she guaranteed the escape of George Washington's ragtag army from the lower city. The Murray Hill section of Manhattan may geographically belong to Midtown, but its spirit has always been more convivial than commercial.

By the late nineteenth century, prominent families competed to live in the Murray Hill area below 42nd Street, a hundred of which were included in Manhattan's first social register in 1892. Mrs. William Astor (Caroline Schermerhorn) led society from her mansion on 34th Street, and John Pierpont Morgan resided on Madison Avenue. The elegant library on 36th Street that bears his name is one of Manhattan's treasures, and its manuscript collections have included two Gutenberg Bibles. Morgan lived in a brownstone townhouse, and blocks of this typical Manhattan family dwelling were soon to rise in every section of the city. Many can be seen in the blocks of the 60s and in the Metropolitan Museum historic district opposite Central Park.

East Side's Turtle Bay area

Today, the East Side denotes wealth, sophistication, and internationalism. Current surveys rank East 57th Street between Fifth and Park Avenues as the most expensive rentable land on the planet. Nearby, the area known as Turtle Bay plays host to the United Nations—the world's legislature and one of the most visited tourist attractions in Manhattan. North of that futuristic complex lies Beekman Place, an area honoring the colonial dynasty whose mansion dominated the area until 1874. It was also the long-time home of

Irving Berlin, the man who "was" American music. Manhattan's East Side also boasts of Sutton Place—a small area of cooperative apartments with extraordinary river views, and perhaps Manhattan's wealthiest enclave since the 1920s. Secretary Generals of the United Nations reside there alongside neighbors who have included such well-known personalities as actors Rex Harrison and Greta Garbo, former New York Governor Mario Cuomo, architect Marion Pei, designer Bill Blass, and publisher Tina Brown.

The primary focus of East Side luxury has long been the "Gold Coast"—the stretch of Fifth Avenue along Central Park that housed the moguls of the Gilded Age as well as today's movers and shakers. Until the 1880s, the largest city homes, constructed for families such as the Belmonts, Havemeyers, Phelpses, and Rhinelanders, were clustered on Midtown's East Side, with their spiritual center in Mrs. Caroline Schermerhorn Astor's mansion on 34th Street. Mrs. Astor determined those who were considered members of "society." Initially, newcomers such as A.T. Stewart and Commodore Vanderbilt were not welcomed, but with half the millionaires in America crowded into Manhattan and eager to flaunt their wealth, such exclusivity did not last. William K. Vanderbilt and his family built French-style chateaux beyond Saint Patrick's Cathedral and literally pulled society north. From the 1880s to 1913, dozens of fine mansions were constructed, and Fifth Avenue became a street for millionaires—a virtual Gold Coast.

Although Manhattan's constantly changing landscape has replaced most of these single-family monuments with apartment houses, a few remain as consulates and museums—reminders of an era of "mad abundance."

Farther to the east, Park Avenue provides another dramatic example of Manhattan's ability to transform itself. Called Fourth Avenue until 1888, the street was more commonly known as the "Avenue of Death" because trains at street level used it to enter Grand Central Terminal. Today, Park Avenue is one of Manhattan's widest streets, covering the railroad right of way that runs beneath the elegant buildings and apartments that line its contemporary borders. The electrified tracks of Metro North run through a tunnel stretching under Park Avenue from 42nd Street to 97th Street, on top of which is found one of Manhattan's most impressive vistas. Saint Bartholomew's Church and the new Waldorf-Astoria existed before World War II, but the construction that turned Park Avenue into a "crystal corridor" of international-style skyscrapers began in the 1950s. Lever House, the Seagram Building, and the Pepsi Building introduced corporate modernism to Manhattan.

Yet amid the glitter of the East Side, neighborhood values endure. Yorkville has been a working-class section of the city since it housed German and Irish laborers who were employed to build Central Park. Manhattan's leading German family, the Rhinelander clan, moved uptown to build a mansion on East 72nd Street, and the following influx made Yorkville more German than Bavaria. Lou Gehrig was born in Yorkville, its ethnic restaurants were famed for beer and game, and its brownstone blocks sheltered solid citizens.

East Side neighborhoods provide a unique aspect of Manhattan's continuing saga because they were dominated by the richest element in the city. The amenities demanded by its residents—the best shops, the finest entertainment, opportunities for art and music appreciation—gave the East Side a glamour it has never lost. ❧

The ballroom of Mrs. Caroline Astor's mansion on 34th Street could hold no more than 400 guests, and so the limit of Manhattan's "high society" was established. [c.1903]

8069. FIFTH AVENUE AND 59 TH. STREET, NEW YORK.

COPYRIGHT, 1904, BY DETROIT PHOTOGRAPHIC CO.

Since 1907, General William T. Sherman has unblinkingly contemplated the hotels and mansions of Fifth Avenue from his secure position at the corner of Central Park. [c.1908]

Fifth Avenue North from 58th St., Approach to Central Park, New York City.

By 1913, the great era of mansion construction on Fifth Avenue was coming to an end, but the Plaza Hotel along with a succession of private homes east of Central Park had already created the Gold Coast. [c.1913]

CARNEGIE MANSION, 5TH AVENUE, NEW YORK

527

When Andrew Carnegie built his "model" mansion on 91st Street, he extended the Gold Coast even farther north. His house became the focus of a neighborhood called Carnegie Hill, and survives today as the Cooper-Hewitt National Design Museum, part of the Smithsonian Institution. [c.1913]

Mansions and Museums

Fifth Avenue runs down the center of Manhattan, a geographic location equally distant from the noise, smells, and incessant activity of both waterfronts. Since the early years of the twentieth century, Fifth Avenue has epitomized both style and elegance. Great department stores clustered there after 1900, but the street's aura of wealth and distinction preceded those retailing empires. It was already the preferred address for the richest families of Manhattan.

For more than a decade after the Civil War ended, Fifth Avenue above 59th Street was nothing more than unpaved ruts. City residents feared it as an area threatened by fever because of its proximity to swampy grounds in Central Park. Building lots were among the cheapest in the city until the 1880s, when attitudes radically changed. The once-ignored stretches of upper Fifth Avenue would be transformed into "two miles of millionaires"—a Gold Coast of wealth that mirrored the excess of America's Gilded Age.

Manhattan society in the 1880s was dominated by Mrs. Caroline Schermerhorn Astor, whose mansion at 34th Street and Fifth Avenue was the heart of elegant New York. North of her home, personages such as William "Boss" Tweed, merchant prince A.T. Stewart, and financier Jay Gould built fine houses, but such men were merely wealthy and not worthy of her notice. Mrs. Astor's social advisor, Ward McAllister, confidently declared there was "no society north of 50th Street." But three unrelated events conspired to shatter that rule: in 1879, Saint Patrick's Cathedral opened; in 1880, the Edison Electric Illumination Co. was chartered; and finally, the Vanderbilt family decided to build beyond the Cathedral at 50th Street. The impressive new Vanderbilt mansions boasted every technological improvement; they demanded attention. When William K. Vanderbilt held an inaugural ball in his new home on March 26, 1883, Mrs. Astor reluctantly attended. Society had suddenly moved north.

In the decades that followed, ambition and the desire for social status, fueled with money gained from the industrialization of the nation, drove mansion building ever northward along the Gold Coast. In 1892, Manhattan was home to approximately 1,800 millionaires—half the richest people in the nation—and in an

In a cumulative effort to move "society" north of 50th Street, six Vanderbilt heirs built homes on Fifth Avenue from 54th to 58th Street during the early 1880s. [c.1902]

age of "mad abundance," each seemed determined to outdo the others. Prominent among those who built French chateaux along the avenue were the Belmont, Clarke, Duke, Flagler, Huntington, Goelet, Rockefeller, Sloane, and Whitney families. Financier J.P. Morgan was one of the few to resist the trend. He refused to move up from his brownstone on 36th Street and Madison Avenue, but did help organize and build the Metropolitan Club on 60th Street for the convenience of Manhattan's elite. Although scores of fine brownstones filled the side streets of the East Side to house the bourgeoisie of the city, metropolitan attention was focused on the spectacle of Fifth Avenue's transformation. And when commercial establishments and hotels invaded lower Fifth Avenue, the movement north accelerated. Even Mrs. Astor joined the procession and commissioned a fine mansion on 65th Street.

Andrew Carnegie made the most dramatic move of all. He ordered the construction of a plain yet spacious house of sixty-four rooms at 91st Street and Fifth Avenue. Farther north than anyone had dared go, Carnegie's "modest" home, the product of a single business deal, became the center of a neighborhood called Carnegie Hill. Not to be outdone, Henry C. Frick, the business associate supposedly outsmarted by Carnegie, bought the Lenox Library on 70th Street and ordered its reconstruction into a mansion that would "make Carnegie's place look like a miner's shack." The architectural masterpiece created by architects Carrère and Hastings became a repository for Frick's art, and was ultimately presented to New York as a "royal gift." Both the Carnegie house and the Frick Collection continue to delight walkers and visitors along Manhattan's "Museum Mile."

Ostentation was characteristic of Gilded Age America, but the passage of the Income Tax Amendment in 1913 curbed such excessive display. Homes with many retainers (Frick's family of three had twenty-seven servants) suddenly became liabilities, and rising real estate values led most of the mansion holders to sell to commercial developers or apartment builders. The great Vanderbilt house on 58th Street became the Bergdorf Goodman department store in 1928. Morton Plant sold his limestone palace to Cartier's (for a two-strand pearl necklace). One of the first Vanderbilt homes beyond Saint Patrick's Cathedral was transformed into a common garment factory. One by one, the monuments of a lost age were replaced, and those that survived were adapted for civic purposes.

Today, the Museum Mile along Central Park includes El Museo del Barrio, the Museum of the City of New York, the Guggenheim, the Jewish Museum, the Met, and the Frick; the Whitney Museum and the Asia Society are nearby. The Willard Straight Mansion long held the International Center of Photography, but, characteristic of Manhattan's constant flux, was reconverted into a private residence. The William S. Miller mansion at 86th Street, originally built for the Vanderbilts, became the latest addition to the Museum Mile in 2001 as the Neue Galerie, devoted to Austrian and German art.

Fifth Avenue's most glorious era still remains visible today. A slow walk along the Museum Mile is still able to evoke the passions and elegance of a bygone age.

Plaza at 5th Avenue and 59th Street, New York, showing Vanderbilt Mansion.

25869

Cornelius Vanderbilt II built Manhattan's largest dwelling occupied by a single family. After his widow sold it in 1925 to obtain tax relief, the site became the Bergdorf Goodman department store. [c.1903]

The Metropolitan Museum of Art

In 1870, members of the Union League Club formed a board of trustees for the creation of a museum of art. It was to be an institution designed to serve as a cultural center for a metropolis of over a million people. John T. Johnston acted as the institution's first president, and his board included prominent members of the artistic community. Sculptor John Q.A. Ward actively helped in the effort to obtain fourteen acres of park on which to build the structure. Collecting art for the museum began in 1871, when Johnston's board acquired a large group of European works and hired art educator George Comfort to organize a curatorial system. The Metropolitan Museum of Art, familiarly called "The Met," also offered classroom lectures around the city to introduce the techniques of fine art to a wide audience.

J.P. Morgan served as president of the Met from 1904 to 1913, and supervised its physical expansion onto Fifth Avenue; additional construction enclosed the original Met building within the larger structure. The firms of Richard M. Hunt and McKim, Mead and White finished the façade, and the museum has been a landmark since 1967. Morgan directed the museum's great expansion of European art holdings, and he donated part of his own collections of medieval and Renaissance works to the museum. He also presided over the first major exposition of American art in 1909, a show that spurred the creation of the museum's American wing, which opened in 1924.

For its first seventy-five years, the Met displayed deeply conservative tastes; its rejection of abstract modern art made possible the birth and growth of the Whitney and Guggenheim Museums, as well as the Museum of Modern Art. Not until 1946 did it acquire its first Picasso as a gift. Thereafter, the curatorial expertise of William Lieberman expanded contemporary holdings so rapidly that the Met became pre-eminent in a formerly ignored area. In the 1960s, director Thomas Hoving began the addition of six new wings, and his "blockbuster" shows, such as the reconstruction of the entire Egyptian Temple of Dendur, drew enormous crowds. The museum became a prime tourist locale drawing up to 5 million persons annually.

With over 2 million works of art and dominance in many areas, the Met is the most prestigious and comprehensive museum in the Western hemisphere, perhaps in the world.

The Metropolitan Museum of Art reigns as the crown jewel of Manhattan's "Museum Mile," and may well be the finest museum in the world. [c.1908]

The Guggenheim Museum

No structure on the "Gold Coast" of Fifth Avenue is more famous or more photographed than the museum honoring the life of Solomon R. Guggenheim. One of seven sons and heir to a great copper and mining fortune, Guggenheim became a philanthropist and gave Manhattan one of its signature buildings.

After business, Guggenheim loved modern art best. He began to show his collection publicly in 1939 at the Museum of Non-Objective Painting, which he sponsored, on 50th Street. In 1943, Guggenheim commissioned Frank Lloyd Wright to create a more permanent home for his art, but the famed architect delayed while he considered sites at the tip of the island and near the Morgan Library on 37th Street. In the meantime, curator Baroness Hilla Rebay moved the existing museum into a Guggenheim mansion at 1071 Fifth Avenue in 1948. Before his death in 1949, Guggenheim acquired a permanent museum site on 88th Street, and provided it with both a building fund and an endowment. His nephew Harry completed the project, and named the museum in honor of his uncle.

The Guggenheim is Frank Lloyd Wright's only important New York structure. He called it a "temple in the Park on the Avenue," but others have likened it to a seashell, a washing machine, a flopped marshmallow, or a sticky bun. The Guggenheim Museum is a concrete spiral rising from a narrow base, a unique shape made possible by steel framing. Wright died six months before the museum opened in October 1959, so he was not able to oppose or oversee the user-friendly alterations that Director James Sweeney made to his design.

For over forty years, visitors have descended the long internal spirals and experienced the entire building as a single gallery of art. Additional galleries were added to the complex in 1972 and 1992, and a SoHo branch existed from 1992 to 2001. Considered both audacious and ambitious, the Guggenheim maintains its reputation as Frank Lloyd Wright's most individualistic work.

The Guggenheim Museum, Frank Lloyd Wright's unique structure on Fifth Avenue between 88th and 89th Streets, is one of Manhattan's signature buildings. [c.1962]

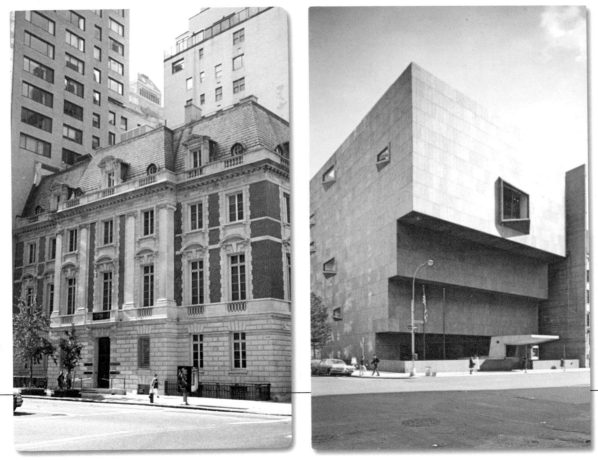

Museumgoers on the East Side can choose from an amazing variety of art experiences. The nineteenth-century elegance of a Vanderbilt mansion has become today's Neue Galerie (left), showing Austrian and German art. [c.2001]

Marcel Breuer's sleek Whitney Museum (right) provides a suitable home for modern painting and sculpture. [c.1968]

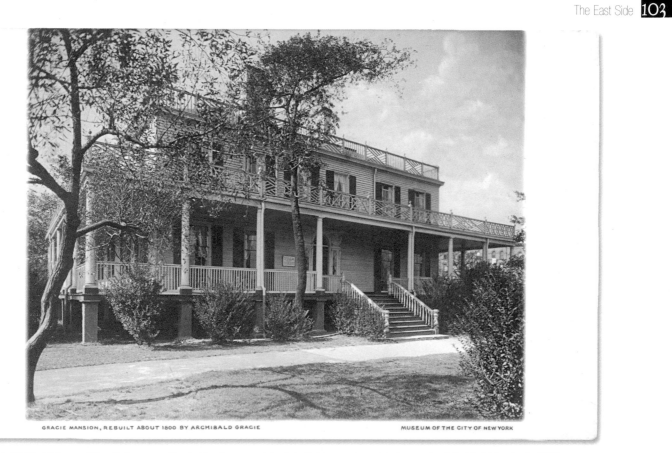

GRACIE MANSION, REBUILT ABOUT 1800 BY ARCHIBALD GRACIE

MUSEUM OF THE CITY OF NEW YORK

The official residence of New York mayors, Gracie Mansion was originally built as a country estate by merchant Archibald Gracie. [c.1930]

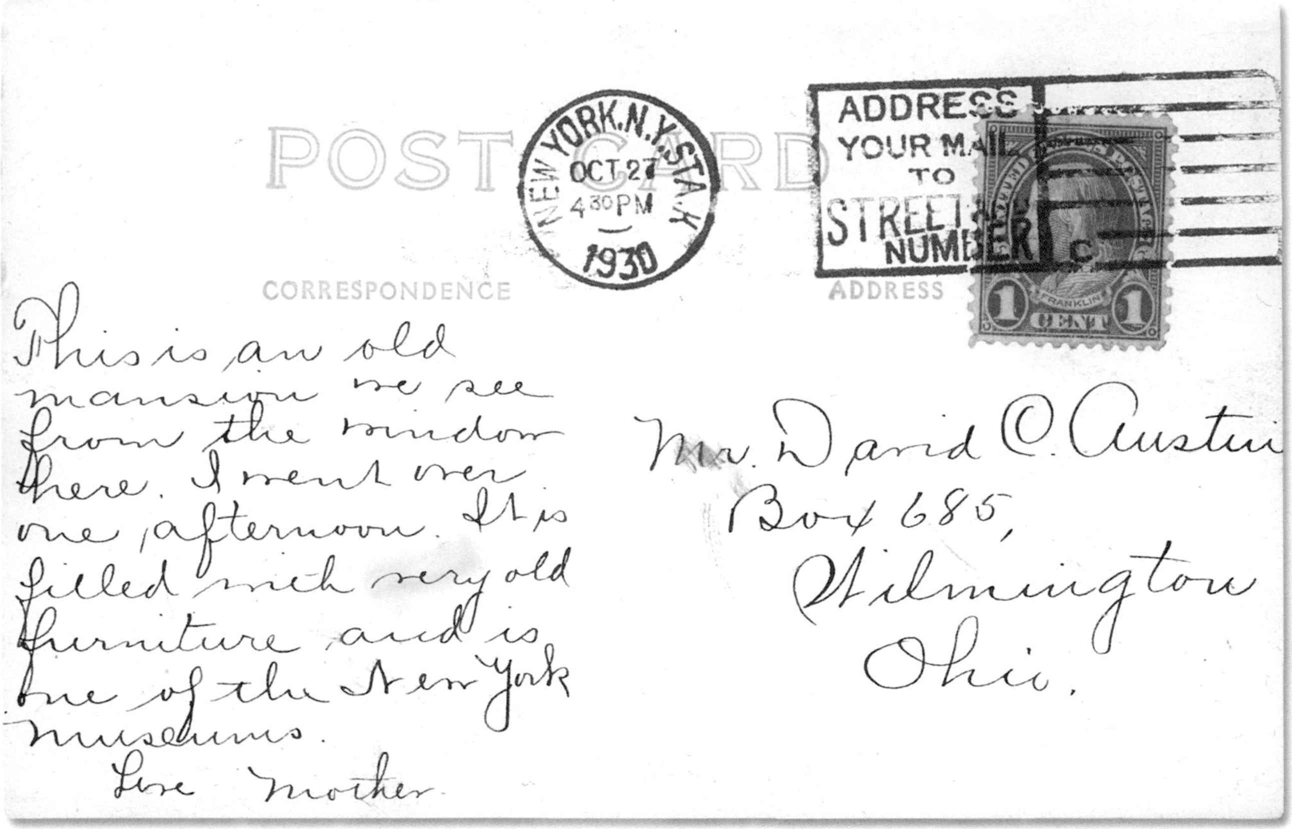
POST CARD

NEW YORK, N.Y. STA. K
OCT 27
4 30 PM
1930

ADDRESS YOUR MAIL TO STREET & NUMBER

CORRESPONDENCE

This is an old mansion we see from the window there. I went over one afternoon. It is filled with very old furniture and is one of the New York museums.

Love Mother

ADDRESS

FRANKLIN
1 CENT 1

Mr. David C. Austin
Box 685,
Wilmington
Ohio.

109A. — East River Drive, Showing Sutton Place, N. Y.   Courtesy — Borough President's Office

Construction of the East River Drive began during the first administration of Mayor Fiorello La Guardia. It was completed on land that had been created out of rubble from London's war-devastated areas. The drive was later renamed FDR Drive to honor President Franklin D. Roosevelt. [c.1943]

COPR. DETROIT PUBLISHING CO

Opened in 1909, the Queensborough Bridge established an automobile route between Queens and Midtown Manhattan. The 59th Street span crosses over Roosevelt Island, once home to city asylums and hospitals—today it is the site of upscale housing. [c.1912]

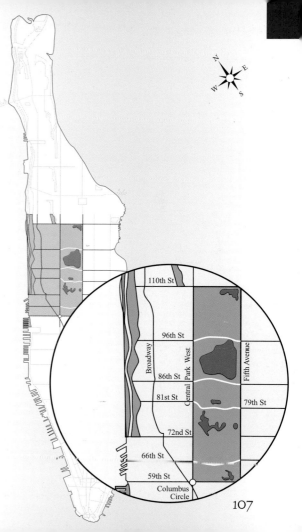

CHAPTER FIVE
The West Side

Contemporary Manhattan offers no more dynamic neighborhood than the West Side. Although the area was once predominantly Jewish, large numbers of Irish, Greek, and Hispanic residents now mingle with tourists on the crowded streets north of Columbus Circle. Gentrification and culture define the West Side, but evidence of its Jewish heritage is provided by the appetizing wonders of Zabar's and the sturgeon available at Barney Greengrass's. These West Side landmarks have today been joined by an unending progression of ethnic restaurants, as well as smart boutiques that fill Columbus Avenue and Broadway. Famed for progressive politics since it voted for Mayor Seth Low in 1900, the modern West Side defines liberalism for a very liberal-minded metropolis.

In 1870, Manhattan was settled only up to 59th Street, and the West Side hardly existed. The area was so isolated and inaccessible that it constituted a neighborhood only in the minds of the most imaginative. The West Side Association had been formed in 1865 to promote improvements west of Central Park, but its only achievement had been to extend horse-car service along the park boundary up to 84th Street. None of the three major avenues that define the modern West Side (Broadway, Riverside Drive, and Central Park West) had even been named at this point. The blocks above 59th Street featured ungraded streets without sewers and scattered shanties filled with squatters. Civilization advanced slowly. In 1879, only The Boulevard (later to become Broadway) effectively cut through the West Side's barren blocks, and perhaps ten paved streets traveled from the park to the river.

Development of the West Side really began after the baleful economic effects of the Panic of 1873 had faded. By 1877, the completion of the American Museum of Natural History and continuing construction of Frederick Law Olmstead's Riverside Drive seemed to indicate better times. Access to the West Side improved in 1879 when the Ninth Avenue elevated railroad reached 81st Street. This was done, obviously, to bring visitors to the museum, but it also encouraged development of upper Manhattan. Institutions and transportation were coming to the West Side, and the people they attracted were soon to pioneer a new lifestyle—apartment living.

The Dakota

As early as 1857, Calvert Vaux, co-creator of Central Park, encouraged city residents to rethink the nature of their homes. "Home" was not necessarily to be defined as a freestanding house, but could be an apartment, as was becoming common in France. But "respectable" New Yorkers preferred private residences to "Parisienne flats," a phrase that carried implications of tenements, adultery, and foreign ways. Not until 1869 did Rutherford Stuyvesant build Manhattan's first apartment house at Irving Place near Union Square; in 1877, its most prominent resident was Mrs. George Custer, widow of the famous American general. By the end of the 1870s, several buildings with multi-room apartments—"tenements for the rich"—such as the Navarre, were clustered in the area directly below Central Park. A family might live in a ten-room apartment there for $1,800 a year, but there was no need yet for such accommodations in the unsettled northwest of Manhattan.

Bringing commodious dwellings to the isolation of the West Side was akin to having pioneers build mansions in the wild. Only a visionary such as Edward S. Clarke, heir to the Singer Sewing Machine fortune, could believe that the West Side deserved elegant apartment houses as well as ordinary three-to-five-story brownstones. The saga of the Dakota apartment house he ordered built on 72nd Street is one of Manhattan's most-told stories—an epic that saw the construction of a fifty-eight-suite palazzo far beyond the limits of civilization. People joked that it was in the wilderness, so a scornful Clarke ordered that the profile of an Indian be sculpted into the façade of his new building. His dream turned into reality, for when the Dakota finally opened in 1884, it was fully rented.

Several of its first occupants were listed in the social register, but most were professional people and businessmen. Newspapers hailed the Dakota as the "largest, most substantial, and most conveniently arranged" apartment house in the world. Clarke, who died of a heart attack before the building opened, had hoped that Manhattan would rename all north-south avenues after western territories of the nation, but this was not to be. His triumph came when future apartment developments honored the Dakota by taking the names Nevada, Montana, Wyoming, Eldorado, and Yosemite.

The Dakota fostered a building boom that soon engulfed the West Side; in 1886 alone, 778 buildings were under construction. By 1910, the area held 3,600 new houses, many of them combination hotel-apartments. From 1904 to 1908, the title of the world's largest residential structure was held successively by the Ansonia on West 73rd Street, the Apthorp on 79th Street, and the Belnord on 86th Street; but literally hundreds of similar buildings were opened. The Ansonia's 350 apartments held 2,500 rooms and, like many West Side buildings, has inspired its own individual monograph. Most important, unlike the private homes that filled Fifth Avenue's Gold Coast, the West Side provided "modest" accommodations for Manhattan's professional, business, and entertainment communities. It is true that mansions existed on the West Side, especially along the Hudson at Riverside Drive, but in time, they too would be replaced by apartment buildings offering the sought after "riv-vu" (river view). Equally, the boarding houses that once filled West End Avenue would be supplanted by fine apartments. The nature of West Side life was determined by its multiple-dwelling buildings.

Gradually, the long-term institutions of the West Side took root. The West End Collegiate Church and its school arrived in 1892, as did the West Side Tennis Club. The Claremont Riding Academy is the oldest in the nation, while the New York Historical Society, established in 1804, traces its roots to the federal period. Old Bloomingdale Road threw off its temporary designation as The Boulevard and became simply Broadway in 1899. In 1902, the West Side received an icon—a forty-foot-tall Statue of Liberty, which is the second largest on earth—when William Flatteau patriotically placed it above his warehouse, a position it held until 2002, when it was moved to Brooklyn. When the IRT subway appeared in 1904, the entire West Side was ripe for settlement and continued population growth.

In the twentieth century, the popularity of apartment houses spread from the West Side across the city. Many of the French chateaux of Manhattan's East Side were replaced by apartment houses, and the settlement of the outer boroughs was also facilitated by the construction of modern high-rises. Once derided as "stacked boxes" or "French shelves," the utility of apartment living on the valuable land of Manhattan was so apparent that 90 percent of island residents were living in such buildings as early as 1930. Apartments remain the preferred accommodation today, although their average size in square footage has fallen greatly and the housing market is cutthroat.

Residents of Manhattan enjoy hearing stories in which a desperate, worthy seeker discovers the "perfect" apartment—one that is convenient, comfortable, and cheap. Most, however, recognize that such stories are usually myths.

131

Columbus Circle and Central Park, New York City

7A-H3147

Columbus Circle, at the intersection of Broadway, Eighth Avenue, 58th Street, and Central Park South, was dedicated in 1892 on the 400th anniversary of the European discovery of America. [c.1930]

From Columbus Circle to Columbus Center

Planners of Central Park were certain that a grand traffic circle would inevitably form at the southwestern edge of their project. They believed the intersection of Broadway, Eighth Avenue, 58th Street, and Central Park South would attract carriages and wagons and cabs as if magnetized, and surely become a vital center of the expanding city. But all West Side development was delayed largely by the economic depression of the 1870s. Eighth Avenue became Central Park West only in 1890, and The Boulevard was not transformed into Broadway until 1899. In that same decade, the traffic circle finally made its impact on West Side life.

Columbus Circle was born on October 12, 1892 when the "Italians resident in America," responding nobly to an appeal by the newspaper *Il Progresso Italo-Americano,* dedicated an 80-foot column of Carrara marble there in honor of Christopher Columbus. Two years later, as traffic surged around the monument, a statue of the great explorer by Gaetano Russo was placed atop. Manhattan's population center was again moving northward. Luxury apartments such as the Navarre Flats had opened nearby and the slums of San Juan Hill, west of the circle, would soon be demolished. All that was needed was a charismatic leader who would turn Columbus Circle into a great public space.

William Randolph Hearst aspired to that role. Publisher of the New York *Journal,* foe of the *World,* and soon to be the instigator of the Spanish-American War, Hearst purchased the Virginia Hotel located south of the circle and transformed it into his newspaper's headquarters in 1895. Hearst believed that Manhattan's expansion would continue and that Columbus Circle was about to boom. He envisioned "Journal Square" as the new center of activity, and purchased as much land in the area as possible. He also sponsored the first Columbus Day Parade in 1900 and opened the Majestic Theater (later the Park Theater) in 1902.

Hearst gambled that the theater district, which had migrated from City Hall to 14th Street to Madison Square and was now in Longacre Square (eventually to become Times Square), would soon arrive at 59th

In the center of Columbus Circle, Gaetano Russo's statue of Christopher Columbus stands atop an eighty-foot-tall column. [c.1905]

Street. He was not alone. Entertainer Gus Edwards built a Music Hall nearby, the Colonial Theater offered prime vaudeville, beer gardens owned by Pabst and Faust opened for business, and Reisenwehr's "lobster house" prepared for enormous crowds. But the theater district stubbornly stayed at 42nd Street and Times Square became the entertainment center of Manhattan. Hearst and the *Journal* sponsored the construction of Harold van Buren Magonigle's Maine Monument—a tribute to those lost in 1898 during the Spanish-American War. The monument was unveiled in 1913 by Hearst's nine-year-old son George. But somehow, Columbus Circle gained only traffic, not prestige, as the West Side grew.

Hearst made Columbus Circle the heart of his publishing empire, constructing his landmark headquarters on 57th Street in 1928, and scattering his many magazines among properties he owned in the surrounding area. But only General Motors followed his lead by placing its headquarters on the circle. Important structures such as Alwyn Court and United States Rubber Building were ultimately built, but the circle's incessant noise and increasing volume of traffic kept additional development away. Gradually, theaters and restaurants in the area closed, and by the 1950s, the Columbus Circle neighborhood seemed tired and run-down—a suitable target for redevelopment by Robert Moses. The movement for West Side renewal brought new buildings, including Edward Stone's Huntington Hartford Gallery in 1964, the New York Coliseum in 1965, and the Gulf and Western Tower in 1970, but these failed to win approval from either the public or architectural critics. The Coliseum was quickly labeled inadequate while the Gulf and Western Corporation sold out to Paramount; the site is currently the Trump International Hotel. The Huntington endured into the new millennium as a "beloved eyesore," incapable of winning landmark status and a perennial target of developers.

In the 1990s, both the Maine and Columbus monuments were refurbished, but a series of ambitious redevelopment plans failed to materialize beyond the planning stage. Only after the Coliseum was razed in 2000 was a plan for enormous 750-foot twin towers designed by David Childs approved for Columbus Circle. When completed, the huge complex—designated Columbus Center—is expected to hold the headquarters of AOL-Time Warner, a Mandarin Oriental Hotel, and numerous restaurants, shops, and residential units. Fitting into the curve of Columbus Circle and opening vistas west along 59th Street, Columbus Center hopefully will bring new vitality to the West Side.

In fulfillment of William Randolph Hearst's dream, his corporation intends to raise a spectacular tower atop his existing headquarters. Since Random House publishers has moved nearby, Columbus Center is expected to become a major media complex. After 150 years, the traffic circle at 59th Street has attained the centrality predicted by the visionary planners of Central Park.

The New York Coliseum at Columbus Circle was never able to accommodate larger conventions and trade shows. Superseded by the Jacob Javits Center, it was demolished by 2000. [c.1966]

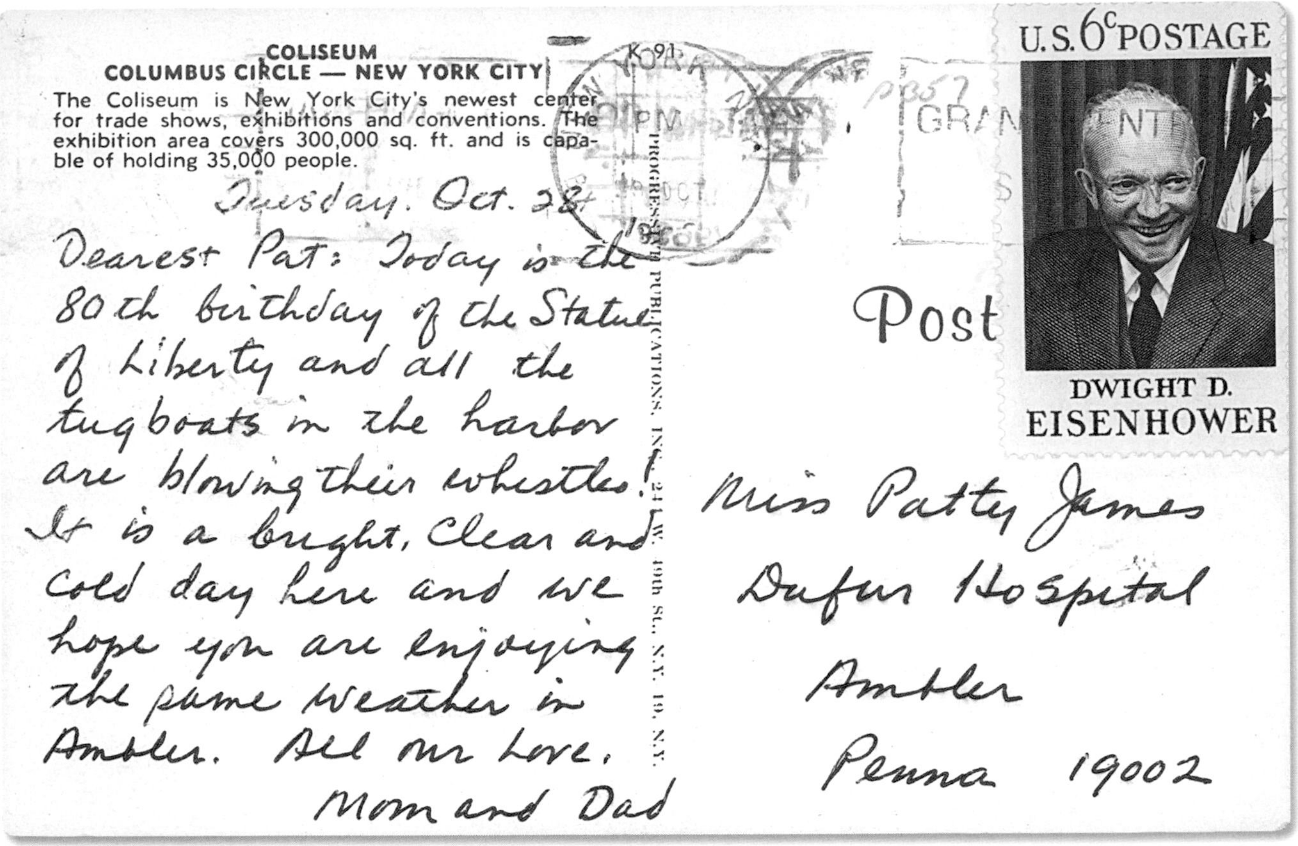

COLISEUM
COLUMBUS CIRCLE — NEW YORK CITY

The Coliseum is New York City's newest center for trade shows, exhibitions and conventions. The exhibition area covers 300,000 sq. ft. and is capable of holding 35,000 people.

Tuesday. Oct. 28

Dearest Pat: Today is the 80th birthday of the Statue of Liberty and all the tugboats in the harbor are blowing their whistles! It is a bright, clear and cold day here and we hope you are enjoying the same weather in Ambler. All our Love.

Mom and Dad

PROGRESS PUBLICATIONS, INC. 24 W. 19th St., N.Y. 19, N.Y.

Post

U.S. 6c POSTAGE
DWIGHT D. EISENHOWER

Miss Patty James
Dufur Hospital
Ambler
Penna 19002

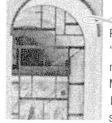

Lincoln Center

Perhaps not even Robert Moses, New York's fabled "master builder," fully anticipated the "cultural supermarket" that would emerge when he began to demolish Manhattan's West Side slum tenements in the 1960s. *West Side Story,* a tragic retelling of doomed lovers, was set in the tenements that fell before his wrecking crews. Out of the debris, Moses built the Coliseum at 59th Street, provided a downtown campus for Fordham University, and facilitated the construction of the world's largest cultural complex at Lincoln Center.

President Dwight Eisenhower presided over groundbreaking ceremonies for Lincoln Center on May 14, 1959, and over the next few years, the neoclassic glass façades of performing arts buildings rose gradually around a public square the size of Saint Mark's in Venice. Max Abramovitz's Philharmonic Hall was completed in 1962, and was joined two years later by Philip Johnson's New York State Theater. The Vivian Beaumont Theater was finished in 1965. The last major building of the complex, William K. Harrison's Metropolitan Opera House, opened on September 16, 1966 with *Antony and Cleopatra,* yet another tale of thwarted love. Gradually, the dozen theater groups that make up "Linc.inc" joined, and in time, the complex offered a cultural mixture that has provided Manhattan with some of its greatest theatrical moments.

Murals by Marc Chagall adorn the Grand Tier promenade of the Metropolitan Opera House at Lincoln Center. [c.1969]

Lincoln Center cost over $180 million to construct, and its existence spurred vast West Side development. Even as the area prospered, the center struggled against poor acoustics in the State Theater, leaky fountains, and critics who berated its design. Like many Manhattan institutions, Lincoln Center became beloved over time, and a series of successful fundraising drives greatly improved the eighteen-acre complex.

When the celebration of the millennium ended, Lincoln Center was to receive a massive refurbishing with estimated costs beyond $1.4 billion. But conflicts between the thirteen component arts organizations at the complex combined with an economic slowdown to prevent rapid implementation of the plan. Lincoln Center, even without new buildings or a covered plaza, remains Manhattan's premier site for the best in opera, jazz, film, ballet, and symphonic music.

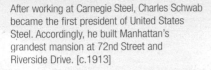

After working at Carnegie Steel, Charles Schwab became the first president of United States Steel. Accordingly, he built Manhattan's grandest mansion at 72nd Street and Riverside Drive. [c.1913]

RESIDENCE OF CHAS. W. SCHWAB, N.Y. CIT

The Ansonia Apartment-Hotel

The Ansonia was the preferred address for Manhattan's musical elite. The building was so well constructed, its apartments were virtually soundproof. [c.1917]

The West Side pioneered Manhattan's vogue for apartment living. The first decade of the 1900s saw the construction of about 4,000 "apartment-hotels" in New York. Many felt that the Ansonia, on Broadway at 73rd Street, was the finest in the city.

The vision of major West Side developer William Earl Dodge Stokes, the Ansonia brought Parisian elegance to Manhattan. Land for the structure was purchased from the New York Orphan Asylum in 1899, but it took five years before the Ansonia opened for tenants. Had it been constructed in Paris, only the Eiffel Tower would have been higher; but in Manhattan, the Ansonia reigned merely as Queen of the West Side. Elegantly attired with a mansard roof, cupolas, turrets, and balconies, the Ansonia offered some unique suites with circular and oval rooms, and almost every apartment provided exceptional views of both city and river. Its three-foot-thick walls were fireproof, and seals were able to swim in its lobby fountain.

In 1906, when Charles Schwab moved into his adjacent mansion on Riverside Drive—the most impressive private home ever constructed in Manhattan—the West Side block between 73rd and 74th Streets became the plushest in Manhattan. Although the Ansonia, dubbed the "most superbly equipped house in the world," was soon surpassed in size, it remained a coveted address. Its first residents paid $1,800 a year for five rooms with a bath, but thirteen-room suites for personages like theatrical producer Florenz Ziegfeld cost $5,000. The apartment-hotel quickly became the center for musical stars—its register listed names such as Caruso, Chaliapin, Elman, Ferrar, Melchior, Pinza, Pons, and Stravinsky. Arturo Toscanini occupied an apartment there for many years, but its single most famous guest was Babe Ruth. The Ansonia served as the inspiration for Saul Bellow's hotel in *Seize the Day,* and bank robber Willie Sutton was once captured in its restaurant. Its Continental Baths nightclub helped launch the career of Bette Midler.

The historical importance of the Ansonia has earned it a listing in the National Register of Historic Places and New York City landmark status. Its interior has been altered, but recent renovations of the exterior restored much of its lost luster. This great lady of the West Side remains uniquely attractive.

The Nevada, Broadway and 69th Street, New York.

The Nevada was the largest apartment-hotel on Broadway in the nineteenth century, but changes in height restrictions in 1901 allowed it to be surpassed by many rivals. [c.1902]

Twin Towers of the West Side

The trauma of terrorist attacks came to Manhattan on September 11, 2001 with an aerial assault that collapsed the Twin Towers of the World Trade Center. Although they are gone, it is somehow comforting to remember that in New York, nothing is ever entirely new or irrevocably lost. On the East Side, Manhattan's first twin towers still stand at Saint Patrick's Cathedral and in the minarets of the Central Synagogue; apartment houses at Ellington Circle and UN Plaza show alternate varieties of the pattern. But the West Side surpasses its cross-park rivals, for a mere twenty-minute walk along Central Park West offers a distinguished series of twin-towered residences.

The West Side attracted bourgeois investors and people in the arts who filled the apartment houses of the growing area. But it was the passage of the Multiple Dwelling Law in 1929 that brought towers to the perimeter of Central Park. This act permitted apartment buildings of up to thirty stories, depending on plot size, if they utilized setbacks. Hungarian-born architect Emery Roth reconstructed the San Remo, located between 74th and 75th Streets.

The Eldorado   The San Remo

The San Remo's success inspired three similar twin-towered clones within fifteen months—the new Eldorado apartment between 90th and 91st Streets, the new Majestic, located across from the Dakota, and the art deco Century at 62nd Street. All of these buildings suffered greatly during the Depression, but each endured to ultimately become expensive co-ops.

The twin towers of these four structures provide a jagged symmetry west of Central Park. The exorbitant prices people pay for their enormous apartments herald a new Manhattan Gilded Age. Dozens of newsmakers reside on Central Park West and walkers sometimes encounter stars on sidewalks. Sadly the twin towers of the World Trade Center, which may have been inspired by the towers on the West Side, are no more. However, the tradition of building "high" remains in Manhattan's lifeblood.

(Far left) The Century. (Left) The Majestic.

The American Museum of Natural History

On December 22, 1877, the American Museum of Natural History moved from its temporary home in Central Park's Arsenal into a new red brick building designed by Calvert Vaux and Jacob Mould. The museum, which fulfilled the vision of founder Albert Bickmore, stood in solitary splendor on Eighth Avenue. Although its land and building belonged to New York, the museum has always been privately administered. The museum, located on 77th Street, was intended to be the first of twelve buildings with four enclosed courtyards, which would have made it the largest public building on the continent. This goal has never been fulfilled, but the twenty-two interconnected structures that constitute today's museum fill half of its four-block site, and welcome over 5 million visitors yearly.

The American Museum of Natural History has undergone continual expansion since the 1890s, and its main entry today is through John Russell Pope's Theodore Roosevelt Memorial on Central Park West. No Manhattan institution can match its proud tradition of scientific research; it includes the work of paleontologists, such as Henry Osborn; oceanographers, like Walter Beebe; anthropologists, including Franz Boas and Margaret Mead; and Africanists, such as Carl Akeley. The museum sponsored Robert Peary's polar expedition and Roy Chapman's excavations in Mongolia. Today, a staff of over 300 continues to expand scientific knowledge in a fashion that

would deeply please Teddy Roosevelt, one of its earliest advocates. The Hayden Planetarium, originally recognized by its Aztec Deco dome, has recently been incorporated into the Rose Center for Earth and Space, one of the most striking and innovative buildings in Manhattan.

Generations of New Yorkers and untold numbers of visitors have enjoyed the American Museum of Natural History, from its dinosaur bones and blue whales, to its war canoes and rare, precious stones. It remains a national treasure and a pillar of Manhattan's West Side.

The firm of Cady, Berg, and Lee created the magnificent Romanesque façade of the American Museum of Natural History. [c.1909]

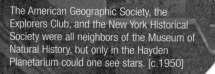

The American Geographic Society, the Explorers Club, and the New York Historical Society were all neighbors of the Museum of Natural History, but only in the Hayden Planetarium could one see stars. [c.1950]

Riverside Drive.   New York.

When Episcopal Bishop Henry C. Potter married socialite Elizabeth Clark in 1901, they moved into her Riverside Drive mansion.
Potter often drove from there to 112th Street to watch construction work on the Cathedral of Saint John the Divine. [c.1904]

Riverside Park, New York City.

© American Studio, N. Y.

Frederick Law Olmstead designed Riverside Drive and Park, artfully shielding residents in mansions and apartments from viewing the unsightly tracks of the New York Central Railroad below. [c.1914]

10747 SOLDIERS' AND SAILORS' MONUMENT, NEW YORK   COPR DETROIT PUBLISHING CO.

Dedicated in 1902, the 100-foot high Soldiers' and Sailors' Monument at 89th Street and Riverside Drive
remains a rarely visited and decoratively incomplete memorial. [c.1919]

CHAPTER SIX
A Walk in Central Park

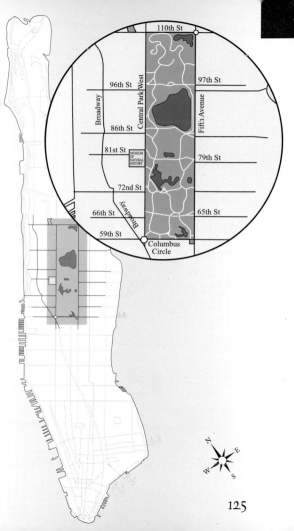

Central Park, 843 acres of natural landscape standing firm against the advance of the concrete city, acts as the lungs of Manhattan Island. It is a living miracle that thrives in a metropolis famed for endless construction and constant change. In the 1840s, when population growth and the stresses of urban living created a longing for green space, Manhattan had fewer than 100 acres of parks for its 700,000 people. This civic deficiency was particularly upsetting to the merchant class—a city elite that had personally experienced the public parks that enhanced London and Paris. They believed that similar amenities were necessary if Manhattan was to secure a position among the world's great cities.

Mr. and Mrs. Robert Mintern became leaders of a movement that endorsed the concept of a single large park, rather than a series of smaller ones for tenement areas. They won editorial endorsement from William Cullen Bryant, editor of the *Evening Post,* and Horace Greeley of the *Tribune,* but their most important supporter was horticulturist Andrew Jackson Downing. Downing was the nation's leading landscaper, one of its first ecologists. In 1851, he wrote a passionate tract extolling the advantages of a large park. But transforming these urban dreams into a reality that would eventually become a national treasure was to take the efforts of many people and decades of work.

Early in the 1850s, Mayor Ambrose Kingsland appointed a special committee to study the park issue, and the group first considered purchasing the Jones Woods picnic area that ran along the East River. But opinion soon swung to support a park five times larger, and in 1853, the state legislature approved Manhattan's acquisition of over 700 acres of land in the center of the island from 59th to 106th Street. It was argued that a centrally located park would stabilize land values, eliminate the scores of squatter families living in Seneca Village around 84th Street, and banish hog farming from the middle of the island.

Both state and city wanted to control park construction and the patronage jobs it would generate. Only after Republicans finally won legislative control did they appoint Andrew Haswell Green to lead the Central Park Commission. Clearing the site began in August 1857, shortly before Frederick Law Olmstead was hired as superintendent. Green's commission then held America's first landscape design competition, selecting, in April 1858, a "Greensward Plan" submitted by Olmstead and Calvert Vaux. Construction would take years, but most major decisions regarding the park were made prior to the Civil War. Additional land purchases in 1863 extended the park up to 110th Street.

Olmstead and Vaux sought to create a natural environment that would provide solace and serenity within the metropolis. To accomplish this goal, they had to reshape the existing land and make nature conform to their vision. Fortunately, the city itself was to the south and there were few buildings on the land allotted for the park. Among still-existing structures that predate Central Park are the Arsenal and the military blockhouse near 108th Street. Workers moved over 10 million horse carts of earth, exploded more gunpowder than was fired at Gettysburg, and planted over a quarter million shrubs and trees (over 334 species) before the job was completed.

Lovely landscapes arose out of the minds of Olmstead and Vaux, and a vast drainage system designed by George Waring was installed to make them viable. At the start of the project in 1857, it was important to show progress; Herculean efforts allowed the "ramble" surrounding Vista Rock to open for walkers late in 1858. When Olmstead's man-made pond near 59th Street opened that winter, it caused an ice-skating craze, which Manhattan still encourages. Olmstead fought constantly with Green over the costs involved, but over the years, a network of open meadows, formal walks, lakes, and woodlands gradually emerged.

Few working people from lower Manhattan had the money or the time to travel up to Central Park, but the more mobile merchant bourgeoisie made good use of its shaded drives. Only late in the century, with the advent of better transportation and leisure Sundays, did the park become available to all residents of Manhattan.

When Civil War halted construction in the park, its rustic future was already threatened. Applications to incorporate "towers . . . cottages . . . gymnasiums . . . Indian work . . . steam-engines . . . fancy dress carnivals," as well as cathedrals and burial sites proliferated. Protecting the natural splendor of the park would become an unending crusade, one of few causes capable of uniting Manhattan's often-warring populations. After 1870, fourteen precious acres of the park were granted to the Metropolitan Museum, and 111 buildings (of which 72 remain) would be constructed across the years; but each of these grants occasioned a fight. Olmstead and the gifted planners he recruited discouraged any intrusions into Central Park. Its primary goal remained sacred—to "dispel from the mind of the visitor, once within its enclosure, thoughts of business and memories calculated to sadden or oppress."

By 1870, the Democratic machine of William M. "Boss" Tweed gained "home rule" authority from the legislature, and took control of park development; its ethos became more democratic. Promenades by gentle folk along its quarter-mile central mall and a daily 4 PM parade of fine carriages dominated park life until a menagerie, a carousel, and donkey rides were added during the 1870s. Sunday concerts were introduced in the 1880s along with playgrounds, tennis courts, and a ball field. Inevitably, millions of annual visits eroded the land, some mayoral administrations neglected maintenance, and buildings constructed along park borders ruined natural vistas. Central Park was only a shadow of its former glory by the 1930s, when Parks Commissioner Robert Moses mobilized an army of WPA workers to restore it. He created the Great Lawn, rebuilt the zoo, and ripped out the casino that had been patronized by Mayor "Jimmy" Walker. He also added twenty playgrounds

Riding through Central Park

and baseball diamonds, and permitted the Tavern on the Green to replace the Sheep Fold. Mayor Fiorello LaGuardia even allowed New Yorkers to sleep on Central Park lawns during heat waves, since the park belonged to the people and there was little fear of crime.

After World War II, Central Park declined once more, a victim of neglect, sporadic funding, and muggings, which gave it a statistically undeserved reputation for violence. City restoration efforts began once again under Mayor Ed Koch and flourished later because of the creation of the Central Park Conservancy in 1979. Elizabeth Barlow Rogers mobilized wealthy supporters living along the park's periphery in support of the public treasure on their front door. The Conservancy, an association of private citizens with public trustees, has spent $250 million to restore the park. Among its accomplishments are refurbished and labeled gates, walks, and benches; the construction of the 2.5-acre Strawberry Fields; a new zoo; a restored Great Lawn; and new landscaping for Cleopatra's Needle, the Shakespeare Garden, and Bethesda Terrace. Most of the park's operating budget and its horticultural maintenance is now handled by the Conservancy, but the group's greatest accomplishment has been to educate the city regarding its grand treasure.

Central Park, both a national and city landmark, is visited by over 20 million people each year. It is Manhattan's finest example of man-made art. ❧

Looking North from Observation Roof, Rockefeller Center

93

16618

The breathtaking splendor of Central Park—verdant greenery amidst the most expensive real estate in the world—is evident in this panoramic postcard. The apartment houses of the West Side and the hotels clustered along Central Park South are prominent elements of the vista. [c.1952]

A horse-drawn carriage ride through Central Park is a traditional part of a visit to Manhattan. An active lobby of animal lovers makes certain that the horses are treated as well as the passengers. [c.1955]

71681 THE PLAZA AND CENTRAL PARK, NEW YORK

Henry Hardenbergh designed the Plaza Hotel, the second to fill the site at the southeastern edge of Central Park. The Plaza retains its Edwardian grandeur after almost a century of catering to its guests, including fictional ones such as those in *Plaza Suite*. [c.1918]

14

COPYRIGHT BY IRVING UNDERHILL, INC., N. Y.

COLUMBUS CIRCLE AND ONE OF THE ENTRANCES TO CENTRAL PARK, LOOKING EAST, NEW YORK CITY

3A-H1277

The Maine Monument, honoring the seamen lost in 1898, is an imposing presence at the Merchant's Gate entrance to Central Park.
Hotels located on Central Park South (at right) provide exceptional views of Manhattan's largest "work of art." [c.1948]

The contrast between the bucolic walks of Central Park and the elegance offered by Manhattan's great hotels is apparent in this view. In the foreground is one of Calvert Vaux's unique bridges, which make strolls in the park so memorable. [c.1948]

SAVOY PLAZA—SHERRY NETHERLANDS AND PIERRE, NEW YORK CITY

3A-H107

Creators of the Park

The Greensward Plan, jointly created by Frederick Law Olmstead and Calvert Vaux in 1858, charted the development of Central Park and has inspired park supporters ever since. Neither of these two men, dominant figures in American landscape architecture in the nineteenth century, was a New Yorker. Vaux was born in Great Britain, came to the United States to work with horticulturist A.J. Downing, moved to Manhattan, and became an American citizen in 1856. Olmstead was the son of a rich Connecticut dry goods merchant who had tried gentleman farming, written a book on the antebellum South, and studied landscaping out of the conviction that nature could help to alleviate the tensions of urban life. On September 11, 1857, Olmstead was named Superintendent of Central Park, but it was Vaux who took the initiative that brought about their professional collaboration. Historians are agreed that neither could have done as well working alone. Together they designed the Greensward proposal that defeated thirty-two other plans, and became the blueprint for Manhattan's greatest work of art.

After 1857, the United States suffered from the effects of a severe recession, so Superintendent Olmstead had no difficulty finding thousands of laborers to clear and level the hills of Manhattan and prepare the site for the park. Olmstead and Vaux waged incessant political, financial, and aesthetic battles. Gradually, armies of workers brought their vision to life. Olmstead hated straight lines. He believed that walking in Central Park should offer new perspectives at the turning of every path, and he was blessed with the ability to see how planted landscapes would look in future decades. He asserted that "every tree and shrub has been planted where it is with a purpose," even installing a giant sequoia, which did not last into the twentieth century.

Olmstead's frequent design changes caused unending battles with Andrew H. Green, Park Commission Chairman from 1857 to 1871. After threatening to quit half a dozen times, Olmstead finally resigned to join the Sanitary Commission during the Civil War, and then spent years in California near Yosemite before return-

Calvert Vaux designed individual plans for each of the thirty-eight bridges in Central Park. His Bow Bridge connects Bethesda Fountain with the Ramble, and may be the most photographed site in the park. [c.1917]

ing to New York. While he was absent, Vaux perfected the system of four sunken transverse roads to accommodate cross-town traffic, as well as an internal circulation system separating pedestrian, horse, and carriage paths. He also completed separate designs for each of Central Park's thirty-eight bridges. The cast iron Bow Bridge between the Terrace and the Ramble is perhaps the most photographed site in the entire park.

Once the partners reunited in November 1865, they continued to create vistas designed to lift the spirit of jaded city residents. *Harper's Weekly* was not alone in proclaiming their work "the finest . . . ever executed in this country," a wonderland where one left the city and drove "into the landscape." The success of Central Park won Olmstead and Vaux planning commissions across the nation. Experts consider their Prospect Park project in Brooklyn an even finer piece of work, but the pair also designed Morningside and Riverside Parks in Manhattan, as well as park systems for Buffalo and Chicago.

Although the Olmstead-Vaux partnership ended in 1872, the two men maintained cordial relations and both vociferously defended the integrity of their work. Olmstead deeply resented any sort of bad behavior in Central Park, and organized mounted rangers to maintain decorum. He bitterly opposed the first children's zoo as a "deduction" from the park, personally axed a baseball diamond, and fought change so vehemently that he was dismissed as superintendent in 1876. Vaux battled just as fiercely but more

subtly, and so was able to oversee not only the construction of his many bridges, but also the Belvedere Castle and the Bethesda Fountain—the largest in Manhattan. The "Angel of the Waters," a statue that presides over the fountain, was created by Emma Stebbins; it was among the first public artworks by a woman. Both men quickly responded whenever threats to their work arose, and their passion has been rewarded—walkers in today's park participate in the vision of its creators.

Vaux remained a lifetime New Yorker, an active member of the city's elite establishment who worked at his profession and contributed to literary magazines. In various partnerships, he designed hospitals and asylums; created a design for Olana, the Hudson Valley home of artist Frederic Church; and even renovated two Gramercy Park townhouses into a home for Samuel J. Tilden. Eventually, this became the National Arts Club. Vaux also collaborated on construction of the Metropolitan Museum of Art and the American Museum of Natural History. Olmstead left New York to live in Brookline, Massachusetts, and designed the Fenway Park system for Boston. During the 1890s, in a last creative spasm, he designed the gardens for Biltmore, the Vanderbilt estate in North Carolina, the largest private residence in the nation. Olmstead battled depression throughout his life, and drifted into dementia during his last years.

Both men provided the nation with an enormous artistic legacy, but their grandest accomplishment remains Central Park.

THE MALL, CENTRAL PARK, NEW YORK.

The "Literary Walk" along Central Park's Mall is one of the enduring treats that draw pedestrians into the park. [c.1906]

CARASOUL, CENTRAL PARK, NEW YORK CITY, N. Y.

Installing a carousel in Central Park was first accomplished in 1872. Generations of Manhattan's children have benefited from this amusement activity amid the trees. [c.1916]

MENAGERIE CENTRAL PARK   NEW YORK.

Central Park built America's first menagerie in the 1870s. Robert Moses rebuilt the zoo in 1934, but the animals often suffered from the restrictions of a caged existence. In the 1980s, the zoo was reshaped into a 6.5-acre natural habitat, and welcomes over a million visitors annually. [c.1905]

Gondolas in Central Park, New York.

Calvert Vaux's Bethesda Terrace and Fountain is one of the focal points of Central Park. [c.1907]

NEW YORK'S
Tavern on the Green
IN CENTRAL PARK

Park Commissioner Robert Moses, who ripped out the casino in Central Park, permitted construction of the Tavern on the Green on the site where sheep once grazed. In 1956, a group of mothers staged a sit-in to prevent a play area's conversion into additional parking for the restaurant. [c. 1939]

The Conservatory, Botanical Gardens, Central Park,
New York City.

Central Park is a continually changing work of art. The Conservatory that once existed there provided plants for the park's walkways. [c.1905]

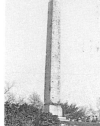

Cleopatra's Needle

Central Park may be a vast tribute to artistic imagination, but its oldest man-made monument was first erected before the Temple of the Sun at Heliopolis, Egypt, around 1475 BC. The red granite obelisk that Manhattan calls Cleopatra's Needle is just over 69 feet high, has an 8-foot-square base, is covered with hieroglyphics, and weighs in at approximately 224 tons. Along with a sister column, this monument was moved to the Caesarian Palace in Alexandria by the Romans in 12 BC, and remained there until the Khedive Ismail Pasha offered it to New York in May 1879.

The obelisk's somewhat smaller sister had been erected with great fanfare on London's Thames embankment in September 1878, and Manhattan eagerly accepted the opportunity to match England's example. Led by Park Commissioner Henry Stebbins, the city decided to place the ancient needle in Central Park on Graywacke Knoll close to the Metropolitan Museum. But dealing with the sheer bulk of the monument would severely test the ingenuity of the metropolis.

Stebbins persuaded William K. Vanderbilt to donate $100,000 to cover moving expenses, and Civil War veteran Henry Gorringe was given the task of delivering the obelisk. Critics on both sides of the ocean accused Gorringe of cultural "vandalism," even as he purchased a steamer, cut a hole in its bow, maneuvered the obelisk inside, and sailed it across the Atlantic. Unloaded in a Staten Island dry dock, the massive stone was floated up the Hudson to 96th Street on the West Side. On September 25, 1880, Cleopatra's Needle began its final voyage of two miles, rolling slowly over a road of cannon balls first to Central Park West, down to 86th Street, through the park to Fifth Avenue, then down to its hilly site. The average daily trip was 100 feet, and the process took over three months.

On January 22, 1881, a crowd of 10,000 people gathered to see the obelisk rise, and a formal presentation to Manhattan took place inside the Met that February. The Met, which holds collections of Egyptian art second only to those found in Cairo, understands that Cleopatra's Needle has no possible connection with the famed Queen, but New Yorkers love it all the same.

Slightly taller and fourteen tons heavier than its sister obelisk in London, this Egyptian artifact has awed Central Park visitors for over a century. [c.1903]

SKATING ON THE LAKE IN CENTRAL PARK
When the ice is four inches thick.

Ice skating has always been a popular city diversion. In this early twentieth-century postcard, the Dakota apartment house overlooks skaters on the frozen lake in Central Park. [c.1907]

C. V. 120. — BOAT HOUSE, CENTRAL PARK, NEW YORK.

"Blue be the skies above you" as this.
May 12th 1907.   Emile.

Boating on Central Park's twenty-two-acre lake has long been a favorite activity for visitors. Park creators Olmstead and Vaux diverted Sawkill Creek and made it the source for the lake, which is a natural stopping point for strollers on the Mall. [c.1907]

Shakespeare in the Park

On summer evenings at 8 PM, magic happens in Central Park. As night descends, a non-existent curtain rises in the park's open-air theater, and gifted actors bring great plays to life; it costs the audience nothing, and is one of the finest amenities of Manhattan. Shakespeare in the Park is one legacy of theatrical genius Joseph Papp, who began to stage Elizabethan plays in an East Village church in 1954, moving his actors outdoors to an East River site in 1956. When the New York Shakespeare Festival was born, Papp often could not even pay his performers. Nevertheless, in 1957 he got a van and announced performances in every borough. Urban legend asserts that his caravan broke down in Central Park, and a troupe headed by Anne Meara and Jerry Stiller played *Two Gentlemen of Verona* on the shore of Belvedere Lake to a cheering audience of thousands. Papp, who was still a stage manager at CBS, had found the perfect home for his Festival, which ran on "2,500 planks and a passion." When Park Commissioner Robert Moses attempted to end Papp's free-admission policy in 1959 because the throngs of people were ruining the lawn, an outraged public sent him bags of grass seed. More important, a judge chided Moses's "arbitrary, capricious and unreasonable" behavior, and dealt the commissioner a rare defeat.

But the grass was indeed "under pressure," and a real stage was needed. George Delacorte, whose philanthropy also gave Central Park its "Alice in Wonderland" statues and a musical zoo clock, provided funding to build an outdoor stage that faced seating in a 120-degree arc. In 1962, CBS televised the Delacorte Theater's first performance—*The Merchant of Venice* with George C. Scott and James Earl Jones. Papp was suddenly the toast of Manhattan. "Theater for all, regardless of ability to pay" made the Festival famous, and Central Park performances helped launch the careers of actors such as Kevin Kline, Meryl Streep, and Raul Julia.

Papp later opened the Public Theater on Astor Place and became a stalwart of the Off-Broadway movement. In 1970, he staged a marathon War of the Roses to raise funds, and launched a full cycle of all Shakespeare's plays before he died in 1991. Attesting to the quality of Papp's legacy, twenty-two plays have moved from the Delacorte and Public Theater stages to Broadway.

Whether seen from the lake or the Great Lawn, Belvedere Castle is one of the focal points of Central Park. It is also where the city's official daily temperature is measured. [c.1900]

Bethesda Fountain, Central Park, New York.

"The Angel of the Waters," a sculpture by Emma Stebbins, presides over the Bethesda Fountain. The "Angel" is beloved, but it didn't hurt that Ms. Stebbins' brother was Parks Commissioner. [c.1908]

SWAN POND, CENTRAL PARK, NEW YORK

1942 ILL POST CARD CO., N. Y.

Central Park has over fifty statues and numerous unrivaled natural vistas, but the cast iron Bow Bridge
is still one of the most photographed sites in the 843-acre preserve. [c.1917]

CHAPTER SEVEN
Manhattan Above the Park

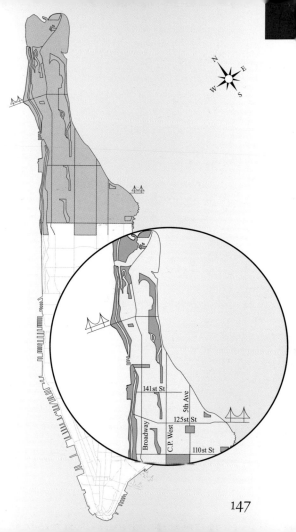

anhattan north of 110th Street has often seemed a foreign land to residents of the lower city, and, until recent years, was rarely visited by tourists who came to the Big Apple. This relative neglect is due to the self-absorption of Downtown, an area whose established leadership believed that there was little of interest above 59th Street. Additionally, twentieth-century New Yorkers shared the belief that upper Manhattan was a dangerous place. Yet the precincts of Harlem, founded by Hendrich de Forest as early as 1637, represent one of the oldest sections of Manhattan. Furthermore, the varied neighborhoods of East Harlem's "Barrio," as well as areas like Inwood, Washington Heights, and Morningside Heights, offer both great attractions and lively histories to visitors.

Director General Peter Stuyvesant chartered the Town of Haarlem on August 14, 1658. Like Haarlem in the Netherlands, it was located only eleven miles from the commercial center, but the American town was so far from the civilization clustered around the Battery that its residents lived in constant danger of Indian attack. Stuyvesant pledged to send a minister and establish ferry service to Harlem's cove, which was near 125th Street, but more often he ignored the settlement.

After the English conquest, Harlem was permitted to keep its name, and gradually its farmers became part of the economic web of Manhattan life. Manhattan's only existing fire tower, built in 1856, stands in present day Mount Morris Park—a height colonial farmers called Snake Hill. A little to the south, the place they named Observatory Hill became the site where Andrew Carnegie would ultimately build his Fifth Avenue mansion.

Harlem was vaguely defined. It included the common land of the East Side above 86th Street, and the Meer Pond, which Frederick Olmstead incorporated into his plans for Central Park. Geographically isolated, Harlem was connected to the lower city only by river ferry and bad roads until railroad service opened in 1837. It then became a Manhattan suburb, filled with mansions and summer homes. Harlem was later the turn-around point where the afternoon carriage drive through Central Park reversed itself.

As the city drove north and elevated train service arrived, developers fostered a building boom in the area above Central Park that resulted in the construction of townhouses as fine as those

South Court, Columbia University

that filled East and West Side blocks. So rapid was Harlem's development that circus owner James Bailey felt it necessary to sell his mansion in 1904 to escape the oncoming tide of people. But the boom collapsed shortly thereafter. As whites lost interest in Harlem, its tremendous inventory of existing apartments drew blacks who were recently displaced from "Black Bohemia" (west of Herald Square) and San Juan Hill (near Columbus Circle), as well as those migrating from the American South. So great was the

influx that apartments had to be divided, and then divided again. Before World War 1, three quarters of Manhattan's black population and all of that community's leadership lived in Harlem—the "Black Metropolis."

In the 1920s, Harlem was the scene of a cultural Renaissance. There was no more exciting place in Manhattan, and nightclubs such as the Cotton Club, Connie's, and Small's attracted crowds from the entire city. But the Harlem Renaissance was far more than clubs and jazz. Writers and artists, such as Claude McKay, Countee Cullen, Langston Hughes, W.E.B. DuBois, James Weldon Johnson, and Zora Hurston walked the streets, found inspiration in their vitality, and chronicled Black America's coming of age. But the Depression and a slide into ghetto status marked the end of that bright dream.

In the nineteenth century, to the west of the Harlem Plain, was the area today called Morningside Heights. Located atop the bluff that ran northward and between Riverside and Morningside Parks were several small villages and two major city institutions—Bloomingdale Insane Asylum and the Leake and Watts Orphan Asylum. Even the Ninth Avenue elevated trains, which made a "suicide curve" at 110th Street over to Harlem, seemed to avoid this area. But at the end of the 1880s, when both asylums relocated northward to White Plains, Columbia University decided to move its Midtown campus north from Madison Avenue to Morningside Heights. President Seth Low engaged the firm of McKim, Mead and White to plan a great campus for the school, and the basis for an "academic acropolis" was created. The Heights was soon to boast the world's greatest concentration of educational institutions, including Barnard College, St. Luke's Hospital, Union Theological Seminary, Jewish Theological Seminary, Teacher's College, Manhattan School of Music, and International House. To accommodate the faculty and students attending these schools, as well as an arriving middle class that sought housing bargains, Manhattan's greatest concentration of twentieth-century apartment houses was constructed on the Heights.

Columbia once planned to build an athletic stadium south of Grant's Tomb, but housing needs of the Upper West Side's growing population forced it to build its famed Baker Field at the north tip of Manhattan. Not surprisingly, the university that was once the landlord of Rockefeller Center also displayed its real estate acumen on Morningside Heights. To this day, it remains the largest landholder on the Heights, even though massive projects such as Morningside Gardens and the General Grant Houses have been constructed in the area. Liberal in its political attitudes, Morningside Heights was always a fully integrated community, yet relations between upper Manhattan's town (Harlem) and gown (academia) were never good. In 1968, long-simmering animosity erupted in a battle over Columbia's plans to build a gymnasium in Morningside Park. Community and student activists forced an end to that proposal, creating tensions that were as high as the 130-foot bluffs that separated the Plains from the Heights. Only Harlem's economic revival in the 1990s eased the relationship.

North of Harlem and Morningside Heights was Manhattan's "final frontier," the last area to be filled by the population of the surging metropolis. Of the many large estates that filled this area in the 1800s, only the Jumel Mansion remains, although the Billings and Audubon estates, bathhouses along the Hudson and Harlem riverbanks, and the Saint George Amusement Park lasted into the twentieth century. The original Highlander Park, where the New York Highlanders (soon to be Yankees) first played, and the Polo Grounds, original home of the Giants, both flourished here. Gradually, Greek and Irish workers filled uptown streets, and the construction of New York Presbyterian Hospital in 1925 provided focus for this neighborhood, which would be called Washington Heights.

Washington Heights provides a clear example of Manhattan's process of ethnic succession, for in the 1930s, Jewish immigrants leaving Harlem or fleeing Hitler became the predominant ethnic group. After the 1960s, the Jewish population was itself displaced by rising numbers of Dominicans, who today feel challenged by a recent influx of Russian and Columbian immigrants. It is a vital community, one that points with pride to the Washington Heights Museum Group, the Cloisters, and Yeshiva University.

Manhattan above the park continues to display the dynamic of social change that is characteristic of the island's history. ✍

One Hundred and Twenty-fifth Street,
West of Seventh Avenue,
New York.

The "main drag" of the Harlem community has always been 125th Street. [c.1903]

Manhattan once hosted seventy-nine breweries, but small manufacturers could not compete with national distributors, such as Milwaukee-based Pabst. Wherever people gathered at night—in Times Square or Columbus Circle or Harlem—there was found a Pabst Beer Hall. [c.1912]

The Apollo Theater

Harlem's most famous theater, the stage "where stars are born and legends are made," began its career as Hurtig and Seamon's burlesque house in 1913. But when the Victoria Theater opened next to it in 1918, the Apollo was no longer the most distinguished playhouse on 125th Street. The theater gradually lost prestige and clientele, and it was not until the Depression, when it changed its name under the management of Frank Schiffman and Leo Brecher, that the Apollo became the place for popular entertainment in Harlem, a virtual community shrine.

Bessie Smith sang the blues on the Apollo's opening night in 1934, and other headliners included dancers such as Buck and Bubbles, Bill "Bojangles" Robinson, and comedian Pigmeat Markham. But it was "Amateur Night" every Wednesday that provided the integrated Apollo audience with its greatest thrills. Ella Fitzgerald won one of the early talent contests there in November of 1934, and later, on the same stage, the illustrious careers of Sarah Vaughn, Flip Wilson, and James Brown were launched.

No theater audience was more demanding. Amateur Night was controlled by members of the demeaning crowd, and such critics as "The Executioner," the "Sandman," and the "Great Adam," rendered verdicts that were final. The Apollo also hosted revues from the Cotton and Ubangi clubs on occasion, and well into the 1950s, presented as many as thirty shows a week. Nat King Cole, Diana Ross, Lionel Hampton, Charlie "Bird" Parker, as well as orchestras led by Duke Ellington and Charlie Barnet appeared there, but it was Amateur Night that people remembered most fondly.

By the 1960s, urban decay engulfed Harlem. Famous stars no longer found it convenient to perform there, and the Apollo was used as a movie theater before going bankrupt in 1981. Purchased by Inner City Broadcasting, the theater received landmark status in 1983. It also received a major renovation before being transferred to the Apollo Theater Foundation. Despite the television syndication of "Showtime at the Apollo" and the active participation of Charles Rangel, Harlem's powerful Congressman, the theater was victimized by financial mismanagement for many years.

Under the leadership of Derek Johnson, the Apollo carried out a major renovation as part of the 125th Street revival. Future plans call for a merger of the Apollo and Victoria theaters, and the creation of a major Harlem theater complex.

Murals in the lobby of the Apollo theater show many of its headline performers, but the most enduring star on 125th Street is the theater itself. [c.1950]

The Hotel Theresa (below) was Harlem's tallest building when it opened in 1913, but unlike the Fane (left), it was racially exclusive until 1937. Fidel Castro enjoyed a memorable stay at the Hotel Theresa in 1960.

FRANK G. LIGHTNER
MANAGER

HOTEL FANE
7 AVE and 135 STREET
NEW YORK CITY

HOTEL

DINING ROOM

23359

Hotel Fane [c.1928]

Hotel Theresa [c.1915] ▶

GRILL, THE WOODSIDE HOTEL, 2424 SEVENTH AVE., AT 142ND ST., NEW YORK CITY

Dining out in Harlem has always provided an opportunity to be seen, as well as to enjoy food.
The Woodside Hotel advertised itself as "the finest for colored people." [c.1935]

COTTON CLUB INC.
"SEARCHY SELLIS - BEN MARDEN
LENOX AVE. & 142 ND ST. N.Y. CITY
DINNING-DANCING-ENTERTAINING
Tel. BRADHURST 1687 AUDUBON 9814

The Cotton Club, perhaps Harlem's most famous nightclub, opened on Lenox Avenue in 1922. Controlled by a notorious gangster, it provided white audiences with elegant revues and entertainment by black performers. [c.1927]

Sugar Ray's Cafe, 2074 Seventh Ave., at 124th St., New York City

THE
SHOW
PLACE
OF
HARLEM

Sugar Ray's

MIKE HEDLEY, MGR.

RAY "SUGAR" ROBINSON

Breakfast—9:30 A.M.   Luncheon—11:30 A.M.   Dinner 4 P.M. till closing

Harlem won fame as a community that deified its sports heroes. American boxer Sugar Ray Robinson often greeted visitors at his restaurant, but spent far more time winning titles. He compiled a record of 114 victories and only 19 losses! [c.1952]

The Second Harlem Renaissance

After World War II, the population of Harlem—the "Capital of Black America"—soared. But conditions deteriorated as southern immigrants continued to arrive, jobs became scarce, and the costs of maintaining rent-controlled property continued to rise. High-rise apartments were soon filled with people on welfare. In time, landlords walked away from unprofitable properties, arson for insurance became common, and the cycle of "urban pathology" seemed to pull down an entire neighborhood. Despite the attempts of Mayor John Lindsay and Governor Nelson Rockefeller to combat crime and drug use with youth programs and office construction, Harlem appeared trapped in a downward spiral. In the face of black progress elsewhere in the nation, it had become a powerful symbol of urban failure. By the early 1980s, New York City held title to 60 percent of Harlem properties.

Yet amid the devastation that consumed two generations, there were always plans for Harlem's restoration. From 1975 to 1985, even as Harlem lost 10,000 units of housing, levels of black income, college graduations, and home ownership constantly rose across America. Eventually, these tangible evidences of gain would have an impact on a community that had excellent transportation access, labor resources, and a vast housing stock. Although Mayor Edward Koch launched a major rehabilitation program, it would take years before home ownership rose and the "main stem" of 125th Street regained its vigor as a shopping center, rather than a place to enter "Bargain World," buy cheap records, or purchase items of "black pride." The McDonald's on 125th Street was the third largest moneymaker in the national chain in 1980, but "Buppies" (Black Urban Professionals) were unlikely to return to Harlem to have a burger. Harlem did not have a supermarket or a good public school, and it was a dangerous environment for children. It needed a "second renaissance."

In retrospect, it seems that Harlem's spectacular turnaround in the 1990s was due more to community spirit than to political intervention. The Harlem Urban Development Corporation, established by New York

Small's Paradise drew audiences with an appreciation for Jazz. The "House of Mirth" attracted headliners from 1925 to 1986. [c.1935]

State in 1970, expired in 1995 with $100 million spent and little accomplished. HUDC had fostered much patronage, but little construction. Famed enclaves such as Strivers Row, Sugar Hill, Sylvan Terrace, and Hamilton Heights had always resisted urban decay. Harlem's more general revival came from the efforts of community groups, like the church-sponsored Abyssinian Development Corporation, which directed rehab and reconstruction work. Dedicated individuals now joined with community groups to use city funding and restore rows of houses opposite Mount Morris Park, as well as on Astor Row, Broadhurst, and Saint Charles.

During the 1990s, rates of home ownership in Harlem almost doubled as gentrification proceeded. One by one, houses were restored to Manhattan's tax rolls, and by 2001, the city owned only 200 Harlem buildings, almost all of which were scheduled for rehabilitation. With more affluent and assured customers, a supermarket returned to the area at 133rd Street and the West Side Highway in 1995. When Pathmark opened a store right on 125th Street in 1999, it was the first Harlem supermarket in fifty years. As final proof of its emergence as a viable place to live, the community was given a separate listing in *Zagat's* 2001 restaurant guide.

Equally impressive is the commercial redevelopment of 125th Street. When the Upper Manhattan Empowerment Zone was created in 1996, some $550 million became available for economic stimulus at the same time that "quality of life" policing tactics began to reduce the incidents of street crime. As both the threat of crime and lack of financial resources eased, Harlem's economy took off. Corporate America suddenly recognized the potential market, and a $68 million shopping mall—Harlem USA—was opened on 125th Street. It includes a multiplex theater owned by basketball great Magic Johnson. Harlem's main street has seen the opening of a Disney Store, Old Navy, and Modell's, while the Business Improvement District has facilitated placement of Met Life, an EAB branch, several clothing stores, a Starbucks, and fast food outlets on the street. In July 2001, former President Bill Clinton moved into offices on 125th Street, and honored a community in which he feels completely at home. The Studio Museum, established in 1968, moved into new facilities here, and the National Black Sports and Entertainment Hall of Fame inducted its first group of honorees. Even the railroad station on 125th Street was upgraded as Harlem came back to life.

For the first time in generations, the mixing of populations that has characterized Manhattan's entire history is evident in Harlem. Since 1980, the Hispanic population of central Harlem has doubled and there are many whites among the families who have rehabilitated brownstones. The vision of an integrated Harlem filled with families who will demand better schools and improved public services is part of a natural growth process that has characterized Manhattan's development since its early Dutch days. Like every other city neighborhood, Harlem benefits from New York's ever-changing kaleidoscope.

Bell Tower, Mt. Morris Park,
New York City.

Bell towers, which provided early warnings of fires until the 1850s, became unnecessary with the creation of the Fire Department of New York and better communication methods. Harlem's bell tower is the last survivor of earlier days. [c.1917]

77 RIVERSIDE DRIVE, GEORGE WASHINGTON BRIDGE AND HUDSON RIVER AT NIGHT, NEW YORK CITY

5A-H647

When it opened in 1931, "George" was the longest suspension bridge in the world. Its steel towers were so beautiful, they were never covered in granite even after a second deck was added in 1962. [c.1938]

Horses and the Speedway

In nineteenth-century Manhattan, great wealth went hand in hand with an appreciation of fine horses. From 4 PM to 6 PM each day, Central Park's East Drive hosted a promenade of carriages—landaus, broughams, and phaetons—a parade of the "well to do." But trotter owners such as "Commodore" Cornelius Vanderbilt, who enjoyed racing his team on Third Avenue, desired speed over pageantry and began to demand a racetrack.

After 1865, horse competitions—called match races—became common on the unpaved streets of upper Manhattan, especially Harlem Lane (now St. Nicholas Avenue). Devotees of the "sport of kings" established the American Jockey Club in 1865, flocked to Leonard Jerome's new racetrack in the Bronx in 1866, cheered at the first Belmont Stakes in 1867, and organized the country's first Polo Club in 1876. In time, the Jockey Club established speed-racing standards for the nation, and William K. Vanderbilt's American Horse Exchange, established in 1881, facilitated the trading and care of fine animals.

SPEEDWAY AND WASHINGTON BRIDGE, NEW YORK

Where the finest horse flesh in the world turn out to speed.

1903. COPYRIGHTED BY A. LOEFFLER.

But as the city grew, unregulated horseracing became dangerous. Despite the presence of six nearby racetracks, in 1892, Manhattan's "horsey" set convinced the legislature to authorize a "speedway" that might be constructed in either Central or Riverside Park. The proposal drew the immediate condemnation of both Central Park designers, Frederick Law Olmstead and Calvert Vaux, who argued vehemently that the parks belonged to all the people and were not playgrounds for the rich. Public opinion forced the elite to retreat, and their attention soon focused on the undeveloped Harlem River waterfront. Designed by C.H. McDonald, the Fort George Speedway opened on July 1, 1898 for the exclusive use of horsemen and trotters in light harness. Extending from 155th to 208th Street, the track featured both a viewing stand and concrete-lined trenches that separated spectators from participants.

In 1900, Manhattan stabled over 100,000 horses, whose owners were powerful enough to have the city temporarily ban automobiles because they frightened horses. Manhattan also suffered the nation's first auto fatality. But cars triumphed with their promise of ever-greater speed, and in 1919, the Fort George Speedway was forced to share the road with cars. Ultimately, this rich man's playground became part of the Harlem River Drive.

Grant's Tomb

After serving two terms as president, enjoying the respite of a four-year world tour, and making an abortive attempt to regain the White House, General Ulysses S. Grant happily settled in Manhattan in 1881. Naïve about business, Grant had lost all his money to a Wall Street con man by May 1884, and faced a bleak and impoverished future. The epic story of how Grant, dying of throat cancer, struggled to complete his *Personal Memoirs,* is justly famous. He dictated his last pages less than a week before he died on July 23, 1885. Published and marketed by Mark Twain's printing company, the *Memoirs* assured the financial future of Grant's family, and is recognized as one of the nation's greatest autobiographies.

Ohio-born Ulysses S. Grant is the only president who is buried in New York City. His tomb was a prime tourist attraction until the 1920s. [c.1922]

Grant loved Manhattan—its clubs, its horseracing, its people—and the city was determined to fulfill his wish to be buried there. His funeral featured a five-hour parade that escorted the body of the fallen hero to a "temporary" vault located near the Soldiers' and Sailors' Monument in Riverside Park; but the General was to remain in temporary quarters for twelve years. It wasn't until 1890 that the building committee finally selected John Duncan to design his tomb. It took no fewer than three separate funding drives to build the 150-foot tomb, which sits on land where the Battle of Harlem Heights was fought in 1776. President William McKinley, joined by veterans from both the Union and Confederate armies, dedicated Grant's Tomb in April 1897.

Grant's Tomb soon became a mecca for tourists in Manhattan, and in the early years of the twentieth century, some 2,000 daily visitors made the long carriage trip up Riverside Drive to view the monument. Land visitors often stopped at the Claremont Inn on Strawberry Hill just beyond the site, and watched as passing riverboat traffic also paid homage to the great general.

Grant's Tomb was one of the most popular tourist attractions in the city, but after its private managers transferred control to the government in 1959, the memorial deteriorated badly, becoming graffiti covered and tragically ignored. In the 1980s, a clean-up campaign led by a Columbia University student restored the site's lost luster but not its popularity. Magnificently located and rich in history, Grant's Tomb is one of Manhattan's forgotten treasures.

The Claremont began its career as the estate of a linen merchant in the 1780s, became a restaurant before the Civil War, and a convenient place for visitors of Grant's Tomb and Riverside Church to watch the Hudson River. [c.1937]

DIRECTION:
ARNOLD SCHLEIFER

A.R.HENNELL

THE CLAREMONT - NEW YORK

CLAREMONT INN — *Direction:* Arnold Schleifer.
Riverside Drive at 124th Street, overlooking the Hudson
River. Original mansion built in 1806. Here the Battle
of Haarlem Heights was fought in 1776.

The Claremont started serving its famous meals before
the Civil War. Today popular priced food and drinks
are served with old time hospitality.

Dancing indoors and outdoors nightly.

POST CARD

Where Paul gave me my engagement ring on the out-door terrace. Aug. 10, 1937.

LUMITONE PHOTOPRINT·NEW YORK·MADE ·IN U·S·A·

Hudson River at Night, New York City

7A-H3775

Hudson River cruises have always been popular. The ship in this postcard is pictured passing in front of Grant's Tomb, Riverside Church, and the Claremont Inn. [c.1938]

The Cathedral of Saint John the Divine

The Episcopal Church played a large part in Manhattan's history, with Trinity Parish vitally influential in developing the lower city. By the 1880s, about fifty churches of that congregation were scattered across the city. On June 1, 1887, Bishop Henry C. Potter announced that an Episcopal cathedral would be built on thirteen newly-acquired acres above Central Park. Potter laid the cornerstone of what would become the largest Gothic church in the world on Saint John's Day, December 17, 1892.

Potter selected the firm of Heins and La Farge to construct a Byzantine-Romanesque church, and the first worship services began in 1899. After Potter's death in 1908, Bishop David Greer changed architects, and the rising cathedral was switched to a Gothic style. After more than a century of construction, the Cathedral of Saint John the Divine remains an unfinished masterwork with a nave that is 601 feet in length, a width at its crossing of 320 feet, and incomplete twin towers that long to pierce the sky. Each of its fourteen bays exalts some aspect of human activity, while its seven magnificent chapels are dedicated to saints and different ethnic groups. Bishop Greer also authorized the placement of additional structures on the grounds, which include the bishop's residence called Synod House, Ogilvie House for the Dean of the Cathedral, and a school. The formal dedication of the Cathedral of Saint John the Divine was held on November 30, 1941, only a week before the attack on Pearl Harbor.

Additional construction halted during the war, but Saint John's was already a fixture of community life in upper Manhattan. Its great bronze doors, featuring sixty Biblical scenes by Henry Wilson, open to serve all. The cathedral's many services include a textile conservation laboratory; a soup kitchen; and memorials to firefighters, AIDS victims, and the Holocaust. Saint John's was a center of opposition to the Vietnam War, and in 1984, it won notoriety by displaying a crucified female "Christa."

Dean James Morton revived the building program in 1979, and stonemasons raised the south tower another fifty feet before construction ended in 1992. In December 2001, a five-alarm fire destroyed a gift shop adjacent to the nave, but the church itself was undamaged. The Cathedral of Saint John the Divine remains Manhattan's largest "work in progress."

The great cathedral's size is best appreciated from a distance. Today it is almost lost in the grid of the city. [c.1911]

"The Cloisters," Fort Tryon Park, New York City

NYC 26

The philanthropy of John D. Rockefeller, Jr. made possible the development of Fort Tryon Park and the creation of a museum within it that is dedicated to medieval art. [c.1939]

POST CARD

THIS SPACE FOR ADDRESS ONLY

SILVERCRAFT—MADE BY DEXTER PRESS, PEARL RIVER, N.Y.

Mrs. M. Blauner,
Crystal Bay
Lake Tahoe
Nevada.

The Cloisters

In the far precincts of Manhattan Island, situated within the famed flowerbeds of Fort Tryon Park and offering unrivaled views of the Hudson, the Palisades, and the George Washington Bridge, is the unique branch of the Metropolitan Museum of Art known as the Cloisters. More than any other part of the Met, it reflects the aesthetic taste and the financial resources of a single patron, John D. Rockefeller, Jr., who virtually willed the Cloisters into existence. Today, it remains the only North American public museum dedicated exclusively to the art and architecture of Europe in the Middle Ages.

In 1914, sculptor George Grey Barnard began to display his medieval art collections in a "cloister" he opened on Fort Washington Avenue at 190th Street. Two years later, Rockefeller purchased 100 Gothic pieces from Barnard, added them to his own collection, and conceived the idea of a specialized museum. World War I interrupted development of the concept, but Rockefeller, whose largesse would restore cathedrals in Rheims and Cologne, as well as create Colonial Williamsburg, revived the plan in 1925 by acquiring Barnard's entire cloister, and then donating it to the Metropolitan.

Beyond that, however, Rockefeller obtained a fifty-six-acre tract of land along the Harlem River that had once been the C.K.G. Billings estate. He gave it to the city in 1930, stipulating that four-and-a-half acres be held as a future museum site. While the city created Fort Tryon Park, Rockefeller hired the English architects Allen and Collens, who had planned the Park Avenue Baptist Church in which he worshipped, to design and build a unique museum. Charles Collens used parts of a chapter house, the ruins of five French cloisters, and a Romanesque chapel, combining them into a single castle-like structure suitable for holding the decorative art of a lost world.

Opened in 1938, the Cloisters displays such medieval treasures as the Unicorn tapestries, Spanish frescos, Saint Edward's Cross, and priceless stained glass. In 1961, the Fuentaduena Chapel was added. Supported by an endowment provided by Rockefeller, the Cloisters successfully transports visitors into a medieval world of craftsmanship, design genius, and extraordinary beauty.

Arcades from the Convent of Trie surround the garden of the Cloisters. Such oases of quiet are rare amidst the constant hubbub of Manhattan. [c.1952]

The Jumel Mansion,
Washington Heights,
New York City.

Built in 1765 as a summer house, the Jumel Mansion was used by George Washington during his attempt to defend Manhattan in 1776. A relic of the eighteenth century, it is supposedly lamented by the spirit of Elizabeth Bowen Jumel Burr, who lived there from 1810 to 1865. [c.1910]

Polo Grounds, New York City.
Home of the New York Giants.

From 1911 to 1957, the New York Giants played baseball at the Polo Grounds, seen here with an inset of manager John McGraw. The stadium was once the largest in the nation, and was home to sports events that still flicker in Manhattan memory. [c.1916]

93   TRIBOROUGH BRIDGE, LOOKING SOUTH FROM OVER THE BRONX, NEW YORK CITY

© INTERNATIONAL NEWS PHOTOS

6A-H1596

The extraordinary complexity of New York traffic and the engineered beauty of Manhattan (at right) is glimpsed in this postcard, which shows the East River; Wards, Randall's, and Roosevelt Islands; two auto bridges; and the rail connection between Penn Station and New England. [c.1938]

𝒞onclusion

𝓜anhattan holds only 7 percent of the land and less than 20 percent of New York City's population. Nevertheless, throughout the twentieth century it has been "the City" both to residents of the outer boroughs and to the rest of the world. From the Battery to Harlem, and from Fifth Avenue to the Cloisters, Manhattan offers a succession of amazing sights that draw over 38 million visitors annually. Its urban texture is known to people around the globe, yet its magnificent buildings and historic importance are only part of Manhattan's allure. The metropolis is the most diverse city in language and ethnicity on earth, and it is an enduring wonder that it functions at all. Everything about Manhattan is stupendous and inadequate. Its harried population exists on the edge of hysteria in an eternal competition for position and business advantage. The congestion on its streets is absurd, housing is always in short supply, and every cab is filled on rainy days. It is a place of blind ambition, intellectual hauteur, and frightening indifference. Documentary filmmaker Ric Burns captured a "mongrel, motley, rapacious city of people trying to get up in life," yet this, too, is only part of Manhattan's story.

Perhaps the greatest marvel of Manhattan is that it is the most tolerant place on earth; a city that is composed of immigrants has to be. Essayist E. B. White found this virtue to be essential, "otherwise it would explode in a radioactive cloud of hate and rancor and bigotry." Despite its attractions and in defiance of its expense, Manhattan thrives because of the people in its many neighborhoods—diverse communities each with individual auras and parochial concerns. The lives of local people intersect on subway and street as they go to jobs, museums, shops, or the waterfront—and the crossings are largely peaceful. No one should be surprised to learn that Manhattan has both the world's largest synagogue and largest Protestant church. It has always been a place of groups and neighbors, all of whom act as if they are alone. Yet the diverse mix unites well enough to make Manhattan the only great American metropolis that has prevented expressways from piercing and destroying its neighborhoods. A strong sense of place and turf permits the larger city to thrive.

Postcards from Manhattan offers a taste of both the elegance and the grittiness of the city, for both of these qualities are part of its never-ending appeal. As the events of September 11, 2001 have proven, structures can crumble, but the spirit of Manhattan's people is indestructible. ✎

The Messages in Print

For the purpose of clarity, each of the handwritten messages found on the postcards has been transcribed and appears below. Minimal clarifications have been made, and are denoted by brackets.

Page 12. *Here we are just landing from Ireland. –M.J.F.*

Page 22. *Well Chas! This is some place. Boy, no place for an Okie! They don't even speak our language. I sure am glad you are at home nice & relaxed. We may go on North or we may come back So. –The Matt Hudsons*

Page 34. *Dear Aunts: If all is good, we will come at noon on Sunday to lunch. With greetings to all. –Finie & Willie (Dear Tanta: Wenn alles gut geht kommen wir bis Sonntag zum mittagessen. Mit gruss an alle.)*

Page 36. *Dear Dolly, will write soon, –Lewis*

Page 51. *Please – stop praying, if you don't, we will all be drowned. –Jack*

Page 54. *We are spending two days in N.Y. –Yours, C.S.M. April 17_07*

Page 76. *Dear Leila, This is where NYs 400 listen to Grand Opera. –With love to all, Your Mother*

Page 89. *Heard "Twain" in this building. –F.H.G.*

Page 94. *I think our last look [is] the very nicest yet, and the one with the best recol[l]ections . . . etc. –A.*

Page 104. *This is an old mansion we see from the window here. I went over one afternoon. It is filled with very old furniture and is one of the New York museums. –Love, Mother*

Page 114. *Dearest Pat: Today is the 80th birthday of the Statue of Liberty and all the tugboats in the harbor are blowing their whistles! It is a bright, clear, and cold day here and we hope you are enjoying the same weather in Ambler. All our Love, –Mom and Dad*

Page 122. *M.D.M. Too bad! Too bad! How very sorry I am the weather proved so unfavorable: and yet how very glad the little fishies must be. I am stoutly at work on Homer. –M. Fri morn August 3, 1909*

Page 138. *To my sweetheart Lulu –From Will*

Page 142. *Dear Babe – Here is where I went skating last winter. Hope you are careful about your medicine and taking it regular yet. –Brother*

Page 143. *"Blue be the skies above you" as this. –Emile May 12th 1907.*

Page 161. *Where the finest horseflesh in the world turn out to speed.*

Page 164. *Where Paul gave me my engagement ring on the outdoor terrace. Aug. 10, 1937.*

Page 168. *Dear Mrs. Blauner, Glad to hear you are all well and that "his royal highness" is working. Have had many nice trips to Jones Beach, Oyster Bay, Briarcliff, Rye, Darien, etc. Am enjoying the Fair. Like going there for dinner and walking. Love to "Schnukel Fritz." Kindest regards to you and Marnie –from H. Sohst*

All numbers that appear in blue type *indicate pages that include postcard images.*

A

Abyssinian Development Corporation, 158

Adams, Abigail, 2

Adams, John, 2

American Museum of Natural History, 108, 120

American Stock Exchange. *See* Curb Exchange.

Ansonia apartment-hotel, 109, 117

Apartment living, development of, 108–109

Apollo Theater, 152

Aquarium, New York, 15, 16

Armory Show, 42

Associated Press headquarters, 82

Astor, Caroline Schermerhorn, 92, 93, 97, 98

Astor Hotel, 78

B

B. Altman's department store, 65, 66

Barnard, George Grey, 169

Bartholdi, Frédéric Auguste, 11

Battery Park, 8, 9, 15

Bedloe's Island, 11

Beekman Place, 92

Bell tower, Mount Morris Park, 159

Belvedere Castle, 144

Bergdorf Goodman department store, 98

Best & Co. department store, 65, 66

Bethesda Fountain, 134, 138, 145

Bloomingdale Insane Asylum, 148

Bloomingdale Road, Old. *See* Broadway.

Bloomingdale's department store, 66

Bogardus, James, 31

Bonwit Teller department store, 66

Boulevard, The. *See* Broadway.

Bow Bridge, 133, 134, 146

Bowery, the, 30, 44, 54, 60

Bowling Green, 8, 17

Broad Street, 23

Broadway, 107, 109, 111

Brooklyn Bridge, 30, 36, 37

Burr, Aaron, 5

C

Cady, Berg, and Lee, 120

Camel sign, 78

Canyon of Heroes, 9

Carnegie, Andrew, 98

Carnegie Hall, 61, 89

Carnegie Hill, 98

Carnegie Mansion, 96, 98

Carrère and Hastings, 80, 98

Cartier, 66

Castle Clinton, 8, 13, 15, 16

Castle Garden. *See* Castle Clinton.

Cathedral of Saint John the Divine, 166

Central Park, 125–146

   Bow Bridge, 133, 134, 146

   Carousel, 136

   Conservatory, 140

   Lake, 142, 143

   Mall, 135

   Menagerie, 137

   Swan Pond, 146

   View from Rockefeller Center, 128, 131,

Central Park Conservancy, 127

Central Park West, 107, 111, 119, 120

Century apartment, 119

Chelsea district, 60, 68

Chinatown, 30, 48, 52, 53

Chinese Mayflower, 48

Chrysler Building, 61, 74, 75

Citicorp Building, 61

City of Greater New York, 3, 30, 37

City Hall, 9, 30

City Hall Park, 36, 39

Claremont Inn, 162, 163

Clarke, Edward S., 108–109

Cleopatra's Needle, 141

Clinton, DeWitt, 16

Cloisters, the, 149, 167, 169

Collect, the, 47, 48

Columbia University, 20, 148–149

Columbus Circle, 110, 111–112, 131

Commissioner's Plan, 59, 60, 85

Constable, Arnold, 65, 66

Cooper, James Fenimore, 13

Cooper-Hewitt National Design Museum, 96. *See also* Carnegie Mansion.

Cooper Union for the Advancement of Science and Art, 45

Cotton Club, 148, 152, 155

Crane, Hart, 42

Curb Exchange, 23

Customs House, 8, 17, 24, 29

D

Dakota apartment, 108, 142

Delacorte, George, 144

Delancey Street, 57

Downing, Andrew Jackson, 125

Dutch West India Company, 7, 13

E

East River Drive, 105

East Side, the, 91–106. *See also* Lower East Side, the.

East Village, the, 31

Edison Electric Illumination Co., 97

Eiffel, Alexandre Gustave, 11

82 Club, 43

El Museo del Barrio, 98

Eldorado apartment, 119

Eldridge Street Synagogue, 48

Ellis Island, 12, 13, 14

Empire State Building, 61, 74, 75

Erie Canal, 2, 41

Erlich's department store, 65

F

FDR Drive. *See* East River Drive.

Federal Court Building, 33

Federal Hall, 24

Federal Reserve Bank Building, 25, 29

Feld, Irving, 70

Fifth Avenue, 61, 65, 66, 77, 92, 94, 95, 97, 98, 99, 101

Fifth Avenue Hotel, 70

59th Street Bridge. *See* Queensborough Bridge.

Five Points district, 30, 47–48

Flatiron Building, 68, 69

Foley Square, 30, 33

Forest, Hendrich de, 147

Fort Amsterdam, 9

Fort George Speedway, 161

Fort Tryon Park, 169

Fraunces Tavern, 9, 18

Frick, Henry C., 98

Frick Collection, 98

Friends of South Street Maritime Museum, 55

Fuller, George, 68

Fuller Building. *See* Flatiron Building.

Fulton Fish Market, 55

Fulton Street, 55

G

Garment Center, 61

General Electric Building, 82. *See also* RCA Building.

George Washington Bridge, 160

Gilbert, Cass, 8, 17

Gimbel's department store, 66

Giuliani, Rudolph, 38

Gold Coast, 92, 95, 96, 97, 101, 109

Gould, Jay, 97

Governor's Island, 8

Gracie, Archibald, 91

Gracie Mansion, 103

Gramercy Park, 60

Grand Central Terminal, 61, 86, 87, 93

Grant, Ulysses S., 162

Grant's Tomb, 162

Great Lawn, Central Park's, 127

Green, Andrew Haswell, 126, 133

Greensward Plan, 126, 133

Greenwich Village, 31, 40, 41, 50

Greer, Bishop David, 166

Guggenheim, Solomon R., 101

Guggenheim Museum, 98, 101

Gulf and Western Tower, 112

H

Haarlem, Town of. See Harlem.

Hamilton Heights, 158

Hansom cab. See Horse-drawn carriage.

Harlem, 147–148, 149. See also Apollo Theater; Cotton Club; Harlem Renaissance; Harlem River Drive; Hotel Fane; Hotel Theresa; 125th Street; Pabst Beer Hall; Small's Paradise; Sugar Ray's Cafe; Woodside Hotel.

Harlem Renaissance, 148, 157–158

Harlem River Drive, 161

Harlem Urban Development Corporation, 157–158

Harrison, Wallace K., 90

Hayden Planetarium, 120, 121

Hearst, William Randolph, 111–112

Hell's Kitchen, 60

Helmsley Building. See New York Central Building.

Herald Square, 3, 61, 64, 66

Hester Street, 46, 48

Highlander Park, 149

Horse-drawn carriage, 129

Horseracing, 161

Hotel Fane, 153

Hotel Pennsylvania, 83

Hotel Theresa, 153

Hoving, Thomas, 100

Hudson River, 165

Hunt, Richard Morris, 11, 100

Huntington Hartford Gallery, 112

Hurtig and Seamon's burlesque house. See Apollo Theater.

I

Il Progresso, 48

Immigration, 13–14

Interborough Rapid Transit (IRT), 42, 85, 109

Iron Palace. See Stewart's department store.

IRT. See Interborough Rapid Transit.

Irving, Washington, 5

J

Jacob Javits Center, 61

Jewish ghetto, 48, 49

Jewish Museum, 98

Johnson, Derek, 152

Jumel Mansion, 149, 170

K

King's College. *See* Columbia University.

Kleindeutschland, 47, 48

Kossuth, Louis, 16

L

Laboulaye, Edouard-René de, 11

Ladies Mile, 60, 65, 66

Lafayette, Marquis de, 16

La Guardia, Fiorello, 105, 127

Leake and Watts Orphan Asylum, 148

Lever House, 74, 93

Lieberman, William, 100

Lincoln Center, 115

Lindsay, John, 157

Literary Walk. *See* Central Park, Mall.

Little Italy, 30

Lord & Taylor department store, 65

Lower East Side, the 47–48

Lower Manhattan, 29–58

M

Macy, Rowland H., 66

Macy's department store, 64, 65, 66

Madison Avenue, 61

Madison Square, 68, 69, 70

Madison Square Garden, 61, 70, 71, 86

Maine Monument, 112, 131

Majestic apartment, 119

Manhattan Bridge, 58

Marble Palace. *See* Stewart's department store.

McAllister, Ward, 97

McKim, Mead and White, 16, 30, 100, 149

Melville, Herman, 5, 41–42

Met, The. *See* Metropolitan Museum of Art.

MetLife Building, modern, 61, 88

MetLife Building, original, 69, 72, 74

MetLife Tower. *See* MetLife Building, original.

Metropolitan Club, 98

Metropolitan Museum of Art, 98, 100, 127, 141, 169

Metropolitan Opera House, 76, 82, 115

Midtown Manhattan, 59–90

MOMA. *See* Museum of Modern Art.

Moore, Clement Clarke, 5, 60

Morgan, J. Pierpont, 20, 92, 98, 100

Morningside Heights, 148–149

Morton, James, 166

Moses, Robert, 16, 42, 90, 112, 115, 127, 137, 139, 144

Mount Morris Park, 148, 158, 159

Mulberry Street, 46

Multiple Dwelling Law, 119

Municipal Building, 30, 33

Murray, Robert, 91

Murray Hill area, 60, 91–92

Museum Mile, 98, 100

Museum of the City of
New York, 98

Museum of Immigration, 14

Museum of Modern Art
(MOMA), 61, 100

Museums

American Museum of
Natural History, 108,
120

Cloisters, the, 149, 167,
169

Cooper-Hewitt National
Design Museum, 96

El Museo del Barrio, 98

Frick Collection, 98

Friends of South Street
Maritime Museum, 55

Guggenheim Museum,
98, 100, 101

Huntington Hartford
Gallery, 112

Jewish Museum, 98

Metropolitan Muscum of
Art, 98, 100, 127, 141,
169

Museum of Immigration,
14

Museum of Modern Art
(MOMA), 100

Museum of the City of
New York, 98

National Black Sports
and Entertainment Hall
of Fame, 158

National Museum of the
American Indian, 8

Neue Galerie, 98, 102

Studio Museum, 158

Tenement Museum, 48

Whitney Museum, 98,
100, 102

N

National Black Sports and
Entertainment Hall of
Fame, 158

National Museum of the
American Indian, 8, 17

Neue Galerie, 98, 102

Nevada apartment, 109,
118

New Amsterdam, 2, 7, 8

New York Central
Building, 88

New York Central
Railroad, 86, 123

New York Coliseum, 112,
113, 115

New York Harbor, 10

New York and Harlem
Railroad, 85

New York Presbyterian
Hospital, 149

New York Public Library,
61, 80

New York Shakespeare
Festival, 144

New York State Theater, 115

New York Stock Exchange
(NYSE), 19–20, 21,
22, 23, 29

New York University, 41, 44

Newspaper Row, 30, 34

NoHo, 31

Nolita, 31

NYSE. See New York
Stock Exchange.

O

Observatory Hill, 148

Olmstead, Frederick Law,
126, 127, 133–134,
148, 161

125th Street, 150, 157, 158

P

Pabst Beer Hall, 151

Papp, Joseph, 144

Paramount Building, 74

Park Avenue, 61, 86, 88, 93

Park Row. *See* Newspaper Row.

Park Row Building, 72

Penn Station. *See* Pennsylvania Station.

Pennsylvania Railroad, 85–86

Pennsylvania Station, 70, 84, 85, 86

Pepsi Building, 93

Peter Cooper Village, 60

Philharmonic Hall, 115

Pier A, 8

Plaza Hotel, 130

Polo Grounds, 149, 171

Post Office, 35

Postcards in America, history of, 4–5

Potter, Bishop Henry C., 166

Prometheus, statue of, 62, 82

P.T. Barnum's Monster Classical and Geological Hippodrome, 70

Public Theater, 144

Pulitzer, Joseph, 74

Q

Queensborough Bridge, 106

R

Radio City Music Hall, 61, 62, 82

Rainbow Room, 82

Rangel, Charles, 152

RCA Building, 75, 82

Riverside Drive, 107, 108, 109, 117, 122, 162

Riverside Park, 123

Rivington Street, 48, 49

Rockefeller, David, 26

Rockefeller, John D., Jr., 82, 169

Rockefeller, Nelson, 26

Rockefeller Center, 61, 62, 82

Roebling, John, 37

Roebling, Washington, 37

Roosevelt Island, 106

Rose Center for Earth and Space, 120

Russo, Gaetano, 111

S

Saint Bartholomew's Church, 93

Saint John the Divine. *See* Cathedral of Saint John the Divine.

Saint Patrick's Cathedral, 81, 97

Saint Paul's Chapel, 24, 29, 35

Saks Fifth Avenue, 66

San Remo apartment, 119

Schermerhorn, Peter, 55

Schwab, Charles, 117

Schwab Mansion, 116

Seagram Building, 74, 93

Sheridan Square, 42

Sherman, General William T., statue of, 94

Shopping in Manhattan, 65–66

Siegel-Cooper department store, 65

Signal towers, traffic, 77

Singer Building, 39, 72, 74

Skyline, 28

Skyscrapers, 72, 73–74, 75, 93

Small's Paradise, 157

Smith, Bessie, 152

SoHo, 31

Soldiers' and Sailors' Monument, 124, 162

South Street museum. See Friends of South Street Maritime Museum.

South Street Seaport, 55, 56

Standard Oil Building, 25

Statue of Liberty, 11, 14, 70, 73

Stebbins, Henry, 141

Stewart, Alexander Turney, 29, 65, 67, 92, 97

Stewart's department store, 29–30, 65

Stone Street Historic District, 8

Straus, Isidore, 64, 66

Straus, Nathan, 64, 66

Strivers Row, 158

Strawberry Fields, 127

Studio Museum, 158

Stuyvesant, Peter, 9, 13, 30, 91, 147

Stuyvesant, Rutherford, 108

Stuyvesant Town, 60, 91

Sugar Hill, 158

Sugar Ray's Cafe, 156

Supreme Court Building, 33

Sutton Place, 92

Swan Pond, 146

Sylvan Terrace, 158

T

Tammany Hall, 38

Tavern on the Green, 139

Tenement Museum, 48

Tenements, 51

Thanksgiving Day Parade, 66

Tiffany & Co., 66

Time headquarters, 82

Times Square, 61, 78, 79, 111–112

Times Tower, 73, 74

Transportation in Manhattan, 85–86

Tribeca area, 31

Triborough Bridge, 172

Trinity Church, 19, 20, 73

Trump International Hotel, 112

Turtle Bay area, 92

Tweed, William Marcy "Boss," 38, 97, 127

Tweed Courthouse, 30, 38

Twin towers of the West Side, 119

Twin Towers of the World Trade Center. See World Trade Center.

U

Union Square, 60, 63

United Nations, 2, 61, 90, 92

Upper Manhattan, 147–172

Upper Manhattan Empowerment Zone, 158

V

Vanderbilt, Cornelius, 86, 92, 161

Vanderbilt, William K., 97, 161

Vanderbilt Mansion, 99

Vaux, Calvert, 108, 120, 126, 132, 133–134, 161

Victoria Theater, 152

Village Voice, 42

Vivian Beaumont Theater, 115

W

Waldorf-Astoria, 83, 93

Walker, Jimmy, 70, 127

Wall Street, 9, 19–20, 74

Wanamaker, John, 67

Wanamaker's department store, 65, 67

Washington, George, 2, 24, 29

Washington Heights, 149

Washington Square, 31, 41, 44

Washington Square Memorial Arch, 44

West Side, the, 107–124

West Side Association, 107

White, Stanford, 44, 70

Whitney Museum, 98, 100, 102

Williamsburg Bridge, 48, 57

W. & J. Sloane department store, 65

Woodside Hotel, 154

Woolworth Building, 29–30, 39, 66, 74

World Trade Center, 26, 27, 29, 74

Wright, Frank Lloyd, 101

Y

Yorkville, 93

OTHER POSTCARD BOOKS *from* SQUAREONE PUBLISHERS

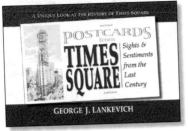

POSTCARDS FROM TIMES SQUARE by George J. Lankevich

Through 130 postcards that span a century, *Postcards from Times Square* paints a picture of an area that has been the home of movie palaces and playhouses, of elite restaurants and fast-food chains, and, eventually, of the best-known New Year's celebration in the world. You'll see the Great White Way exchange its gaslights for electric bulbs and, eventually, for neon. You'll visit famed sights like Roseland, Radio City Music Hall, and Sardi's. And you'll discover how this world-renowned landmark has weathered a tumultuous century, growing from its rural roots, achieving worldwide fame, suffering a twilight of decay, and, ultimately, recapturing its magic.

$14.95 • 192 pages • 8.5 x 5.5-inch quality paperback • NYC/Collectibles/History • ISBN 0-7570-0100-9

POSTCARDS FROM WORLD WAR II by Robynn Clairday and Matt Clairday

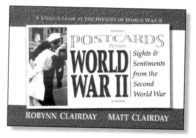

Postcards from World War II offers an invaluable collection of postcards that were sent between 1941 and 1945. Through their images and messages, these cards offer a unique glimpse into the everyday lives of the servicemen and women who lived during this historic fight for freedom. The postcard was a quick, convenient means for soldiers to communicate with distant loved ones, and no matter what the message, each card was a way of saying, "I'm okay." In a world of doubt and devastation, it was an affirmation of life. *Postcards from World War II* helps recapture the triumphs and the tragedies of this time. Each postcard is truly a part of our collective American history, a tangible memory of the heroism of the "greatest" generation.

$14.95 • 192 pages • 8.5 x 5.5-inch quality paperback • Collectibles/History • ISBN 0-7570-0102-5

POSTCARDS FROM SANTA CLAUS by Robert C. Hoffman

In *Postcards from Santa Claus,* author Robert C. Hoffman presents a collection of over one hundred beautifully colored picture postcards that trace the development of Santa throughout the last century. From the turn-of-the-century Santa to the Santa of the roaring twenties to the Baby Boomer Santa, we experience a unique visual history of this Christmas icon. In addition to pictures, the book shares with its readers personal messages of love, well wishes, and joy—frozen in time. Throughout are insets that highlight fascinating Santa trivia such as the origin of the Santa legend; the creator of the Santa we see today; Santa's names around the world, and much more. For those who love the spirit of Christmas, *Postcards from Santa Claus* can evoke wonderful holiday memories all year round.

$14.95 • 192 pages • 8.5 x 5.5-inch paperback • Full Color• ISBN 0-7570-0105-X